praise for *The Gift of Self-Love*

"Mary reminds us that one of the kindest acts of self-care involves tuning out the pressures of the outside world and learning to appreciate ourselves for who we truly are."

SHANNON KAISER

author of *The Self-Love Experiment* and *Joy Seeker*

"This workbook is filled with actionable advice that will actually help you put self-love into practice (the most important part!). This book will help you work through the beliefs and expectations that have kept you stuck, and help you realize that you are wonderful exactly as you are."

CAROLINE DOONER

author of *The F*ck It Diet*

"Through a lens of Intuitive Eating and Health at Every Size, Mary has written a supportive, encouraging book to help you fight diet culture and come to a place of gratitude for the mere existence of your body. By relating to her personal story, Mary will help you see that you're not alone in your struggles with food and your body and will give you the courage to make the changes you need to live a trusting, sensual, and meaningful life. I highly recommend this beautiful, compassionate book for all who need a guidebook toward self-appreciation and self-love."

ELYSE RESCH, MS, RDN, CEDRD-S

nutrition therapist and author of *The Intuitive Eating Workbook for Teens* and *The Intuitive Eating Journal—Principles for Nourishing a Healthy Relationship with Food*; Co-author of *Intuitive Eating* and *The Intuitive Eating Workbook*

"For topics so nuanced, despicably monetized, and often traumatizing, Mary tackles body image, diet culture, and self-acceptance masterfully. She seamlessly weaves together data, anecdotes, and poignant questions to paint a picture of what self-love could look like in the real, everyday version of our lives if we're brave enough to reach out and take it."

ZOE MARSHALL

TV writer and producer

"Mary has written a game-changing book that will change the lives of so many women! She bravely tackles the topic of radical self-love and how that can and will impact any woman with body issues (all of us!) but especially women struggling with eating disorders. This book gives people permission to embrace their bodies and love themselves for who they truly are."

REGENA THOMASHAUER

author of *Pussy: A Reclamation*

"In this relatable and practical workbook, Mary helps move people from disempowering self-criticism to renewed self-love."

KARA LOEWENTHEIL

J.D., M.C.C., host of the *UnF*ck Your Brain* podcast

the gift of self-love

A WORKBOOK TO HELP YOU BUILD CONFIDENCE, RECOGNIZE YOUR
WORTH, AND LEARN TO FINALLY LOVE YOURSELF

Mary Jelkovsky

Design by: Megan Kesting
Cover Art by: Sabina Fenn

ISBN 9781950968275

Printed in Mexico

10 9 8 7 6 5 4 3 2

DISCLAIMER:
This book is for informational and educational purposes. Please consult your health-care provider before beginning any health-care program.

to my two best friends:
Mama & Ilana

table of contents

i feel you, babe.

Do you ever find yourself caught in a negative thought spiral that tells you you're just not enough?

Not skinny enough. Not pretty enough. Not fit enough.

Not smart enough. Not accomplished enough. Not confident enough.

Not a good enough mom or wife or daughter or sister or friend.

Do you ever feel like you can't shake these thoughts, no matter what you do?

Despite knowing better, do you find yourself mindlessly scrolling through Instagram, comparing yourself with all those super gorgeous lifestyle bloggers and wondering what they even do for a living? Or maybe to that popular girl from high school whose life still looks perfect? Or to those moms who manage to always look rested, put together, and dress their kids in the cutest outfits? If your answer is yes to any of those, I have one thing to say: I feel you, babe.

I used to struggle with these feelings all the time, and to be honest, sometimes I still do. I think we all do. Sometimes these thoughts are short lived, slipping away as fast as they came. But other times, the feeling of not being enough can linger for days or even weeks. Sometimes you get so used to feeling bad about yourself that you don't even notice that it's been a few years since you actually felt good. That critical voice inside your head constantly reminds you that you aren't enough and then tells you that you'll never be enough until you …

Lose those last 10 pounds, get rid of your baby weight, or tone your arms some more. Get a promotion, a raise, or a bonus. Cook a delicious, yet healthy, meal for your family and pack perfect lunches for the kids, preferably the night before, because that's what good moms do, right? Learn another skill that will let you change your resume from "intermediate" to "proficient." Do your makeup and get your eyebrows waxed, eyelashes filled, and nails done. Find a significant other and get married, plan the perfect wedding, and then throw the perfect cocktail parties, just like your ex–best friend from high school (thanks, Facebook, for throwing those photos in my face!). After that, buy a nicer car and a bigger house, and after that …

Look, I get it. For years, I thought the solution to "not being good enough" was to simply have more and do more. I thought if I just worked harder on myself, then I would have more to be happy about, which would eventually make me feel better about myself as a whole.

But the trick with this kind of thinking is that it never ends. And guess what? No matter how much weight I lost, how many nice things I bought, or how much I accomplished, that underlying feeling of not being enough didn't go away. If anything, it got worse over time.

Eventually, I had to find another way.

my story

As a first-generation American from an immigrant home, I did everything I could to become the person my family wanted me to be: a girl who checked all the boxes, met all of society's expectations, and looked perfect while doing it. And on the surface, that's exactly what I appeared to be. I was an ambitious, high-achieving, and self-motivated student with a full-ride scholarship to college, and I had the kind of looks that rarely left me without a date. Some would say I was "the perfect girl."

Nevertheless, I was fighting a war inside my mind: never feeling good enough. Not smart enough. Not thin enough. Not pretty enough. Not accomplished enough. Simply not enough. I honestly thought that I didn't feel like I was enough because I wasn't doing enough. So I kept pushing myself to the limit—and past the limit—in a desperate attempt to feel better. On top of my academic achievements, I started competing in bikini fitness competitions, thinking that if I had the "perfect body" and won a trophy to prove how dedicated, disciplined, and determined I was, then I would finally be happy with myself. But no matter what I did, there was still that critical voice inside my head.

Despite having an average-sized body, I still worked to lose weight, but it was never enough. (Hello, body dysmorphia!) I was good at school, but not as brilliant as the girl sitting next to me in calculus. (Hello, comparisonitis!) I constantly sought validation from men and women alike and did anything and everything I could to get everyone to like me. (Hello, people pleaser!) But no matter how many people liked me, I never felt lovable, because I couldn't … love … myself.

Self-love was a foreign concept to me. I thought it was just for people who were either born super pretty, confident, and popular or achieved very little and used self-love as an excuse to give up on themselves. But my big secret was that I envied anyone who looked like they loved themselves, because that kind of happiness felt totally out of reach, like one more thing I wasn't good enough at.

It never clicked in my head that the weight loss, compliments, and attention were not helping me. If anything, they were adding fuel to my self-destructive fire. All of it made me feel good in the moment, but then the feeling would quickly fade away, and I would find myself back in a cycle of self-loathing and striving all over again.

Have you ever thrown newspapers into a firepit? The fire gets very big, very fast from the paper burning but then dies back down a few seconds later. Well, weight loss, compliments, and attention were the newspapers to my internal flame. It was easy to throw them in there and start a fire, but it would die out quickly and ultimately leave my light dimmer than it was before.

I call this the self-loathing cycle. For example, many people think *If only I could change my body, then I'd be happier with myself.* So you go on a diet, the diet fails you, and you get into this terrible cycle of restricting your food → "losing control" and binge eating → feeling ashamed → hating yourself → bingeing a bit more → starting again on Monday, swearing this time will be different → and doing it again from square one. Even if you do lose weight, you'll find something else about your body that needs to be changed, because it's never enough.

Or maybe you think that if only you had more money, then you could afford a nicer house or that fancy vacation. So you work harder and buy those nice things, but the satisfaction is so short lived because it's never enough. And if you're anything like me, you may have fallen into the trap of thinking that once you achieve that career milestone or life goal, you'll finally feel successful. But then you see someone else who seems to be doing so much "better" than you, so you set another goal, create another plan, and add more things to your to-do list, because it's never enough.

The worst part is, this cycle has become so normal.

The "GO, GO, GO! ACHIEVE, ACHIEVE, ACHIEVE!" messages are everywhere. Productivity has become the new badge of honor; if you're not always being productive, you feel like you're failing. Exhaustion is now hailed as an accomplishment. (How many people at your work brag about being tired?) There always seems to be something more to work toward: more likes, more recognition, more efficiency, more activities, more money, more stuff, and more of whatever else you think you need to feel happy.

I'm not saying that you shouldn't work hard toward your goals, but it's very difficult to overcome your insecurities, be at peace with who you are, and learn how to love yourself when you fill every minute of your day and continually run yourself ragged.

Learning how to love yourself requires you to slow down. It takes a lot of deep self-exploration and often uncomfortable work. And that's exactly why I wrote this book: to make this self-love journey as simple as possible for you, so you don't spend another minute trapped in the vicious, self-destructive cycle of not feeling good enough.

side note: As an able-bodied, cisgender, white woman, I recognize that I hold a lot of privilege in this world. I had access to education and resources that set me up for success, and I was never discriminated against for the color of my skin, my body size, or my physical abilities. That's not to say that my life was easy, but rather that I was born with certain advantages that many marginalized people do not have. As I share my internal struggle with self-love, I am aware that my struggle was, in fact, internal, and that I did not have to face much of the stigma, oppression, and discrimination that marginalized people face everyday. Although social justice is just as important, this book focuses mainly on the inner journey to self-love. I hope that no matter your background, this book helps you recognize that you are worthy of everything good in the world, no matter who may think or say otherwise.

this book will not fix you,
.... # because you were never broken ....

When the cycle of not feeling good enough spins out of control, you can be left feeling broken. When I first realized how badly I was struggling, I went to my doctor, thinking (read: hoping) that all my sadness was due to a hormonal issue. I begged her to fix me.

I would also call my best friend and hope she'd say something that would make me feel better. I thought maybe her nice words could cheer me up, but they never did. No matter what anyone said, I still felt lost and hopeless. I was waiting on someone—anyone—to do something to fix me or say something to make me feel better.

Then I went to see a counselor, told her everything I was feeling, and said, "I know I have a lot of issues. Can you fix me?"

She shook her head and said, "No, I can't fix you, because you are not broken."

I didn't understand her at the time. I thought that if I felt broken, I must be broken. But as I came to learn, and as I'll share with you in this book, your thoughts and feelings are not the truth. They're your truth in the moment (which is totally valid), but they are not the cold, hard truth.

It didn't occur to me back then that no one could make me feel better, because all the answers were within me. If you're rolling your eyes, thinking, *Oh God, here she goes with some spiritual woo-woo stuff,* I get it. I used to think that too!

As cliché as it sounds, all the answers are already within you, and nobody can fix you or make you feel a certain way, because you are not broken.

You were never broken.

And you will never be broken.

Sometimes you may feel broken, which is OK. Everyone feels broken sometimes.

And sometimes, when you feel like you're breaking down, you're really breaking open. With every crack, you create space to hold more experiences, more knowledge, and more wisdom about yourself.

Everyone goes through different things in life, and you're probably harder on yourself than you are on others. You are not alone. You are not flawed, damaged, or stupid for feeling a certain way. You are human—a full, whole, and complete human being.

i'm not here to fix you but rather to guide you so you can reconnect with your true self: the woman who respects, accepts, and loves herself.

Much of my self-love journey came about while I was healing from an eating disorder, so throughout this book, I share personal stories and breakthroughs related to diet, weight loss, and body image. But every day I realize more and more that how you feel about your body is only the tip of the iceberg on this journey. So even if you've never struggled with food or your body, you will still get a lot out of this book.

You will learn how to approach your needs with self-compassion, practice positive self-talk, and reframe how you see, think, and feel about yourself. The following pages will give you new perspectives and a balanced approach to self-love, with topics including intimacy, relationships, forgiveness for body image, pleasure, and mindset. With every story or idea, there is an exercise, either a written self-reflection or a self-love challenge, which is intentionally crafted to help you put the ideas into practice.

how to get the most out of this book

In the following chapters, you'll find a mix of tips, tools, research, pep talks, challenges, exercises, and inspiration to help you love yourself. As you dive in, take it one concept at a time. Don't rush. Read the words on the page and let the messages sink in. Take as much time as you need to think about how my story relates to yours and how you can apply the self-love lessons to your personal journey.

Then, DO THE WORK. (You'll come to learn that all caps = Mary is very serious.) You MUST do the work to be successful in changing your mindset. If you don't do the work—skipping over the self-love challenges or journaling exercises—then your feelings about yourself won't change. You can read all the inspirational quotes and attend all the empowering seminars you want, but if you don't use these tools in your daily life, the positive effects won't stick. Please do the work for the sake of your own healing.

As you're going along, bookmark (or take photos on your phone and save) any pages you want to refer back to or remember. This book is yours forever. It's meant to be written in, highlighted, annotated, cried on, carried with you, and cherished. After all, your self-love journey is a serious, important, life-changing matter, so go ahead and pour your heart out on the pages that follow.

I'm confident that if you commit to this journey, read carefully, and do the exercises intentionally, then you, too, will experience a self-lovin' transformation beyond your imagination.

are you ready?

~~~

Remember: There's no such thing as being somewhat committed. You either are or you aren't. There's no in-between. But once you're committed, your transformation will begin.

1. do you want to reframe your mindset to see yourself in a more positive light and learn to love yourself for who you are?

◯ *yes* ◯ *no*

2. are you committed to doing the work it takes to get there?

◯ *yes* ◯ *no*

your self-love vision

Your Self-Love Vision is your mission statement—your guiding light—for how great life will be once you embrace loving yourself. Ask yourself the questions below and write your vision on the following page.

〜〜〜〜

✦ **what does self-love look like to you? be specific!**

✦ **how do you want to feel about yourself?**

✦ **what things do you see yourself doing once insecurities don't get in your way anymore?**

✦ **what clothes will you wear (or not wear!)?**

✦ **what will your relationships be like?**

✦ **what bold career moves will you make once you realize how capable you are?**

This is your Self-Love Vision. Because in order to get anywhere in life,
you need to have a vision of where you are going.

_____
_____
_____
_____
_____
_____
_____
_____
_____
_____
_____
_____
_____
_____
_____
_____
_____
_____
_____
_____
_____

↑ **fill up the whole page and don't hold back!**

part one

loving yourself

chapter 1
the self-love formula

♡ + XO = SELF-LOVE

the self-love formula

I don't know about you, but growing up I completely lacked conversations about the importance of self-love. The only time I remember even seeing the phrase was in a little Buddhist meditation book that I picked up at a bookstore when I was 15. I don't even remember what the book said about self-love because the phrase itself held no meaning to me. It didn't even capture my attention.

Self-love seemed like this thing that everyone was supposed to have, but that no one really knew how to achieve. If anything, self-love just seemed like it had to do with loving your body, but as I'll address throughout this book, self-love goes so far beyond our bodies.

Eventually, I looked up "self-love" in the Merriam-Webster Dictionary. That's when I discovered that it's classified as a noun and defined as "an appreciation of one's own worth or virtue" and "proper regard for and attention to one's own happiness and well-being."

Self-love is definitely about tending to our worth, virtue, happiness, and well-being. But as I've progressed on this journey, I've realized that it is so much more than a noun. Self-love is a verb—it's an action, a choice, a process. It's about the choices we make and the steps we take each day to make ourselves feel loved.

In practice, self-love will look different for everyone. Sometimes it's about staying in to do some studying, pleasure reading, or simply sleeping when your friends are begging you to go out. Other times self-love is about challenging yourself to take a risk and talk to the cute barista at the cafe because you know you need to put yourself out there. Sometimes it will be about doing those clichéd things like taking a bubble bath or getting your nails done. The best way I can sum it up is that self-love is about saying YES to yourself, even when it means saying NO to others. In this chapter, we'll explore a deeper, more holistic definition of self-love.

first, just be.

Before you put pressure on yourself to do a ton of things to show yourself love, though, you first have to make the decision to BE more loving toward yourself.

What does it mean to be loving toward yourself? Well, let's use your relationships with others as a point of reference. Think about it: Your friends or significant other don't always have to DO things for you to make you feel loved. Most of the time, just being there for you is enough. And the deeper your relationship gets, the more all the little things about them—their hugs, their care, their gestures—mean the most. In the same way, a deep, loving relationship with yourself is about constantly being loving toward yourself and making yourself a priority.

The first step is making the decision that you're going to BE loving toward yourself from here on out. Then, ask yourself what that means to you. For instance, when I love someone, I try to listen to them and validate their feelings. I also put extra effort into making the other person feel seen, heard, and appreciated. I spend time with them. I love them just as much (if not more) in their difficult times as I do when they're happy. I do little things to make them feel good, like giving a long hug, offering words of encouragement, or sending a thoughtful text. The way you love others can give you clues for how to love yourself.

Your relationship with yourself is just like any other relationship. In order for it to be a good, healthy, and loving relationship, it requires quality time, compassion, intention, forgiveness, and loving energy. Listen to yourself. Offer yourself support and encouragement. Give yourself what you need. Keep your promises to yourself. Take yourself seriously. Make yourself feel important. Spend time with yourself. Love yourself even when you're not feeling lovable.

Likewise, if you want to BE more confident, you don't have to DO anything first. It's not about focusing on all the things you need to HAVE (like money, time, resources, or stuff) before you can DO the things you want to do (like travel, start a business, or find the love of your life). Before any of that, you first need to BEcome the most empowered version of you, whatever that looks like to you. Make the decision that from here on out, you're committed to BEing a confident person and BEing loving toward yourself. The rest will follow.

who do I want to be?

Below, list 5 words that describe your best personality or who you want to BE. Think about how you want to show up in this world and how you want to be remembered by your loved ones. These should be positive words like kind, confident, authentic, inspiring, empowering, compassionate, passionate, creative, connected, loving, and so on.

1. ....

2. ....

3. ....

4. ....

5. ....

now, take a moment to tell yourself that you can already BE these things, starting now.

list one thing that you think would help you BE, or embody, each of the five words you wrote.

For example, "I can BE authentic by being my true self around my friends and whenever I'm meeting new people."

1. i can BE .... **by . . .**

....

....

2. i can BE .... **by . . .**

....

....

3. i can BE .... **by . . .**

....

....

4. i can BE .... **by . . .**

....

....

....

5. i can BE .... **by . . .**

....

....

Now let's form a more well-rounded definition of self-love, one that feels more tangible, practical, and relevant to all areas of life.

When thinking about self-love as a whole, I see it as having three main parts: self-esteem, self-worth, and self-compassion. This is what I call the **Self-Love Formula.**

self-esteem + self-worth + self-compassion

A lot of people use these words interchangeably, but there are a few critical distinctions. Learning their individual meanings will help you organize your thoughts and feelings and commit more fully to self-love on all levels. Let's dive in!

self-esteem: being confident

Self-esteem is probably what comes to mind first when you think of self-love. But what exactly does it mean?

Self-esteem is how you think of yourself as a person. If you generally believe you're a good person who deserves good things, then you have high self-esteem. People who have low self-esteem tend to believe they are inferior to others. Self-esteem is something everyone has. Some have it more than others, but there is no human being with zero self-esteem. It's not possible, because part of being human is having thoughts and feelings about yourself, and these can vary throughout your life.

Confidence is the belief in your own abilities. It's similar to self-esteem but more circumstantial. For example, you can feel confident or sure of yourself at the office but lack confidence when it comes to expressing yourself in the bedroom. Your confidence levels vary depending on what you're doing. Understanding this distinction means that you can no longer say you're "not a confident person."

Read that again—and then again.

Confidence is not about who you are as a person, but your lack of confidence in one area of life (like your relationships) may trickle into other areas of your life and cause you to feel less confident in others as well. That's when your confidence can start to affect your self-esteem—how you think and feel about yourself as a whole.

But it doesn't have to be that way. You can acknowledge and admit to yourself something like, *Hey, I don't feel really confident in my body, but I feel pretty confident at work.* Even a simple distinction like that allows you to be real with yourself about your specific strengths and struggles without letting them dramatically affect your overall self-esteem.

Even though self-esteem is more generalized than confidence, they are proportional to one another. The more you build your confidence in specific areas, the better you'll feel about yourself and the more self-esteem you'll have in general. And the more self-esteem you have in general, the more confident you'll feel about your specific abilities. Throughout this book, I use "confidence" and "self-esteem" interchangeably, because while they technically have different meanings, they are intrinsically linked.

Another common misconception is that confidence is about how good you are at something. People assume that if you're skilled at something, then you must be confident about it. But you know what it's like to have someone tell you you're really good at something and then not feel that way yourself.

In their book *The Confidence Code*, authors Katty Kay and Claire Shipman found a pretty big "confidence gap" between women and men. Women are less sure of themselves, even when they are just as competent, qualified, and capable as their male colleagues. A study done by two psychologists, David Dunning from Cornell University and Joyce Ehrlinger from the University of Washington, gave male and female college students a pop quiz on scientific reasoning. The students were asked to rate how confident they were in their scientific abilities on a scale from 1 to 10. Women gave themselves an average score of 6.5, and men, 7.6. Then Dunning and Ehrlinger asked the students to predict how confident they were that they got the questions correct. Women gave themselves a 5.8 out of 10, on average, while men gave themselves a 7.1.

How well did they actually do?

About the same. Women scored a 7.5 out of 10, and men scored a 7.9. But women underestimated their scientific abilities as a whole and were 22 percent less confident in their quiz answers than their male peers.

Columbia Business School even came up with a term for this: "honest overconfidence." Statistically, men have much more of it; on average men rate their performance to be 30 percent better than it is. Even from personal experience, I know that I'm much more likely to underestimate my abilities than overestimate them. I often find myself (over)thinking and questioning if I'm smart enough, qualified enough, or good enough, whether it involves speaking up in a meeting or writing this book.

Note: Although Columbia Business School doesn't specify, I take it that the study was done on cisgender people who identify as either a man or a woman. The concept of confidence is likely more nuanced and complex for those who do not fit into the gender binary, such as transgender or gender-fluid people.

In summary, confidence is not about your actual abilities but your belief in your abilities. It's about believing you are capable of taking on new challenges, trying new things (even when you're not that good at them yet!), and doing anything you set your mind to.

how confident are you?

Here is a little quiz to help you see where your confidence falls in different areas of life. For each of these statements, rate yourself from 1 to 10, with 1 meaning not confident at all and 10 being completely confident.

1. romantic relationships:

I can comfortably express myself in my romantic relationships, because I know that what I have to say matters. If I'm not in a relationship, I enjoy my own company and have fun dating whenever I feel like meeting new people.

2. family:

I can comfortably express myself to my family, because I know that my feelings are valid. I know that there is no such thing as a perfect mom/daughter/sister/partner/spouse. I do my best, and I know that my best is good enough.

3. friendships and social life:

I can comfortably be my true self around my friends, because I know they love, value, and appreciate me for who I am.

4. career, business, and work:

I feel sure of my abilities at work or in my business. I believe I am capable of taking on new projects, learning as I go, and overcoming challenges along the way.

5. finances:

I know I deserve to be compensated accordingly for my work and that I deserve the money I make. I am comfortable in my financial status and feel I am on the right track toward financial stability or financial freedom.

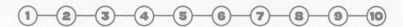

6. physical health:

I treat my body well and keep myself healthy to the best of my abilities. I trust, appreciate, and listen to my body and give it what it needs.

7. mental and emotional well-being:

I am proactive with my mental and emotional well-being by speaking kindly to myself, treating myself as I would someone I love, and asking for help when I need it.

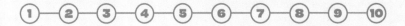

8. spirituality:

I keep an open mind when it comes to spirituality, knowing that even though I don't know everything, I am entitled to my own beliefs. I feel at peace with my relationship with my god, my subconscious, and the universe.

my results: ....

✦

Your confidence in each area is simply wherever you fall on that scale from 1 to 10.

Your self-esteem is all of those ratings added up and divided by eight (eight categories).

I don't want you to beat yourself up about any of these quiz results. That would totally defeat the purpose of this book! This quiz is simply meant to help you become aware of how you feel about your life, where you struggle with confidence, and where you are on your self-love journey. Think of it as a good starting point for getting to know yourself better.

self-worth: being enough

Self-worth is linked to any time you hear that word "enough" in your inner dialogue. Maybe you're getting ready for a date and you think, *Ugh, I'm not pretty enough,* because your hair is a bit frizzy. Or your baby is throwing a tantrum and you find yourself wondering, *What if I'm not a good enough parent?* Or you achieved a milestone in your career like a new job or a promotion, but you find yourself wondering, *Am I qualified enough for this? Do I really deserve it?* Or maybe you lost a few pounds, but you still find yourself thinking, *It's not enough. I just need to lose a few more, and then I'll be happy with my body.* Or you and your significant other get in a fight and you take everything they said to mean, "You aren't good enough!" The list goes on and on, but whenever you catch yourself thinking or feeling "not enough," it's a signal that you're struggling with self-worth.

Write this statement down seven times on the lines below:

i have enough. i do enough. i am enough.

_____

_____

_____

_____

_____

_____

Self-worth is about who you are rather than what you do. You'll notice with the above examples that the inner dialogue about self-worth is very personal. It's not just that you don't like your hair; it's that not having perfect hair means you don't feel pretty enough as a whole. You don't recognize that your baby is just being fussy; you believe it's a reflection on your parenting and, therefore, you. You don't give yourself credit for getting that high position at work; instead, you question whether you deserve it. You forget that it takes two to tango in a relationship, and you blame yourself when really, the situation is much more nuanced than that.

A lot of people use self-worth and self-esteem interchangeably, but I like to think of self-worth as existing on a deeper level. Remember how self-esteem is dependent on your thoughts, feelings, and judgments? Well, having high self-worth means knowing that regardless of how you think about yourself, you are still fundamentally valuable as a person.

Having high self-worth, on the other hand, is knowing that regardless of how you think about yourself, you are still fundamentally valuable as a person. It's independent of your thoughts, feelings, and judgments. It's recognizing that your value is intrinsic, and no matter what mistakes you make or how you feel about yourself at any given moment, nothing will change your innate value as a human being.

self-esteem vs. self-worth	
"I am good at this."	"I am a good human."
"I look good today."	"My value does not come from my appearance."
"I feel good about myself today."	"I am good even when I don't feel like it."
"I am enough because..."	"I am enough."
"I am worthy because..."	"I am worthy."

Basing self-worth on external factors—how you look, how much money you have, how many people give you compliments, how much approval you get from others—is the fastest road to low self-worth, because, like I said, nothing external can change your internal value as a person. The more you try to replace your internal value with external validation, the unhappier you'll be.

The only thing that can make you feel worthy and good enough is consciously recognizing that you already are worthy and good enough, because you're a living, breathing human being who deserves love, respect, and good things in this life.

That's it, you win! Cue confetti!

self-compassion: being kind to yourself

Imagine if I called you on the phone right now and said, "You know that guy I went out with last night? He flat-out told me that he doesn't think we're a good match, and now I'm devastated because I really liked him!"

Would you roll your eyes and say, "Mary, it's probably because you gained weight recently and have that pimple on your chin. And that dress you wore on your date? Let's just say, I'm glad you didn't ask me if you looked fat in it, because I wouldn't have been able to lie! Also, you talk too much, and everything you say is kind of boring, so it doesn't surprise me that he doesn't like you. You should give up on dating now, because you'll probably be alone forever anyway!"

YOU. WOULD. NEVER.

You would never say that to your friend! You would never even say that to a stranger!

You've heard how you should treat yourself as you would someone you love, so why do you continue being so freaking hard on yourself—w-a-a-a-ay harder than you would ever be on a dear friend?

Well, it's simply because you were never taught to treat yourself with love. You were taught the Golden Rule—"Do unto others as you would have them do unto you,"—but no one ever preached, "Treat yourself how you want others to treat you."

Self-compassion is about giving yourself gentle love and kindness no matter what you've said or done. It's a practice that's there for you no matter what happens externally.

Self-compassion is what you need on those days when you're feeling drained and exhausted from work, unmotivated to clean the house, or insecure because the person you like is not texting you back.

It's not about ignoring those low feelings, but rather it's about allowing yourself to feel them and speaking to yourself with kindness as you move through them. It's about reminding yourself that these feelings are completely normal—that everyone feels this way from time to time—and that feeling "less than" at any given moment does not mean you are a lesser human being.

Self-compassion is about being kind to yourself on both good days and bad days.

The common stereotype behind self-compassion (much like self-love) is that too much of it will make you lazy, complacent, and unmotivated. In reality, the opposite is true. Dr. Kristin Neff, a pioneer in the field of self-compassion research, has found that self-criticism taps into the body's threat-response system (also known as your reptilian brain), making your stress levels go up and taking a toll on your mental, emotional, and physical well-being. Constant self-criticism can lead to chronic stress, anxiety, and depression. And I don't know about you, but when I'm constantly feeling stressed, anxious, or depressed, I'm definitely not productive. Sure, you can force yourself to stay busy and try to "prove" yourself to other people, but over time, that will leave you more tired, bitter, and disconnected from yourself.

Self-compassion, on the other hand, serves as an intrinsic motivator, because it comes from your mammalian brain, or limbic system, making you feel nurtured and cared for. As a result, oxytocin and endorphins (also known as the cuddle and happy chemicals) are released in your brain, which help combat negative feelings and allow you to happily move on with your life. Just think how much easier it is to get stuff done when you feel excited, motivated, and passionate about what you're doing. Self-compassion allows you to tap into those positive emotions, making your life much, much easier than when you try to criticize yourself into "doing better."

An important component of self-compassion is using mindfulness to put things in perspective. This helps you escape catastrophic thinking and remember that you have agency, or control, over your circumstances. It's not about telling yourself that you're perfect no matter what. Rather, it's about validating your feelings and giving yourself permission to learn from the experience you're having without letting it define you. Self-compassion isn't saying, "I'm a failure." But it also isn't saying, "I never fail." Self-compassion is saying, "I tried and failed at that task, and that's OK. Everyone fails sometimes. It's how I'll grow."

self-criticism vs. self-compassion

Here are some other ways to shift your inner dialogue from self-criticism to self-compassion. Think of your own example for how you can reframe it with compassion for yourself.

self-criticism

1. If I fail, it means there's something wrong with me.

2. They don't like me because I'm _____. I need to change so I can be more likable.

   I'm a mess. I can't do anything right.
3.

   I'm a bad person.
4.   .
   I'm so stupid.
5.
   I'm not a good enough employee/mom/
6. sister/friend/daughter/wife/business owner/person.

   Why do I always do this?! I should know
7. better by now.

self-compassion

1. Failure is a part of growth.

2. Not everyone is going to like me, and that's OK. Being the best version of myself will always attract the right people, who like me for me.

3. I'm human, and I'm allowed to make mistakes.

4. I did something I'm not proud of.

5. I am learning.

6. I am enough just as I am, and nothing can alter my worth as a human being.

7. I am doing the best I can with what I know.

Notice how self-compassion also has critical aspects of building self-esteem and recognizing your intrinsic self-worth. All three parts of the self-love formula—self-esteem, self-worth, and self-compassion—intertwine, working together to form a holistic approach to self-love.

〜〜〜

get real with how you feel so you can heal

Now that you know what self-esteem, self-worth, and self-compassion mean, what part of the Self-Love Formula are you struggling with most right now?

self-esteem

self-worth

self-compassion

And if you're struggling with more than one, or even all three, that's totally OK! It's why you're here, on this journey to self-love.

Think about your answer and all the different areas of your life. Now write down everything you're feeling, struggling with, or want to work on. Remember, self-compassion is about validating your own feelings, no matter how unpleasant they may be. Once you admit all your negative thoughts, feelings, and emotions, it'll become much easier to deal with them, because you will have gotten them out of your head and onto paper.

_____

_____

_____

_____

_____

_____

_____

_____

_____

_____

_____

_____

_____

_____

_____

_____

_____

_____

_____

_____

_____

_____

_____

_____

Write a letter of self-compassion to yourself. What would you say to someone you deeply care about if they were dealing with the same struggles? What advice would you give them? How would you make them feel better? Now do that for yourself.

DEAR ME, _____

_____

_____

_____

_____

_____

_____

_____

_____

_____

_____

_____

_____

_____

_____

_____ ♡ Me

Self-love is not about doing everything in the Self-Love Formula perfectly but becoming more aware of how you think and feel about yourself so that eventually, you can see yourself in a more positive light.

······························ **your self-love promise** ···························

Your self-love promise is your commitment to this journey. Some days, keeping this promise will feel harder than others, but again, this isn't about being perfect. It's about making a conscious effort. Once you make your self-love promise, there is no going back, because you've already opened the door to what it's like to love yourself—fully, wholly, and unconditionally!

Rewrite the statement below on the next page. Sign your name.

i promise to be more loving toward myself, even when it's difficult.

i promise to believe in myself, even when my self-esteem feels low.

i promise to remind myself that i'm worthy, even when i don't feel like i'm enough.

i promise to practice self-compassion, even when i don't think i deserve it.

i promise to be more loving toward myself, because i am deserving of my own love.

my self-love promise:

X _____

XOXO

chapter 2
the self-love pie

the self-love pie

I was recently at my family's house when my mom told my 11-year-old sister, Ilana, to clean her room. Ilana (who considers herself a "craftlete" because she loves arts and crafts so much) said, "Mama, it's not my fault I'm messy! It's because I'm so creative!"

My mom rolled her eyes, but her slight smile gave away that she was inspired by my sister's response. So was I. In this simple statement, my sister revealed her self-awareness, confidence, and ability to find gifts in her imperfections. A big part of self-love is learning to accept, and even embrace, your so-called "flaws," because they usually also contain your most extraordinary gifts.

My sister also demonstrated the power of shifting your perspective. You can spend time focusing on and criticizing your drawbacks, or you can make the choice to acknowledge them, give yourself credit where it's due, and love yourself through it. If this sounds daunting, just remember that if my little sister can do it, so can you. Learning to love yourself in different areas of life is the goal of this chapter.

The most important thing to remember is that self-love will look different for everybody. The ways I need to love myself may differ from the exact ways you need to love yourself. To better understand this, I'll go through what I call the Self-Love Pie, which breaks down the areas of life where everyone needs self-love. First, though, let's address some common misconceptions about self-love that might be getting in your way.

is self-love selfish?

The biggest myth out there is that self-love is selfish. Far too many people think that if you love yourself "too much," you'll turn into a narcissistic asshole. It's what I believed most of my life, and then, in an attempt not to turn into a narcissistic asshole, I adopted a practice of self-hate instead. I decided that not liking myself was a form of humility.

Over time, I came to realize that hating myself was what actually made me a narcissistic asshole, because I was constantly thinking about myself! Whether it was about having the perfect body or being the perfect student, I was trapped in my thoughts of never feeling good enough and always wanting to be better.

Think about it: When you hate yourself, who are you thinking about all the time?

YOURSELF.

I didn't share my gifts with the world, because I thought I had nothing to offer. I wasn't present with my little sister, because my mind was always focused on what I was going to eat next, and I was so physically exhausted from hours of exercise that I didn't have any extra mental or emotional energy to give her. I was constantly worried about whether other people liked me, instead of focusing on the people who LOVE me unconditionally.

There's nothing humble about not liking yourself. It causes you to be preoccupied with your insecurities and prevents you from living in the moment. It also requires tons of energy and takes you away from the people who love you. Plus, when you're so focused on your own shortcomings, it's way too easy to miss the gifts in others.

Self-love, on the other hand, expands your capacity to love from the inside out. Once you fill yourself with self-love, that love will spill out to those around you. So, no, self-love is not selfish. It's generous and expansive.

Here's the secret: When you truly love yourself, you actually won't think about yourself very often.

if i like myself too much, will
i get fat, lazy, and ugly?

We live in a society where everything is about go, go, go; do, do, do; succeed, succeed, succeed. And when we're not going or doing or succeeding, we're busy worrying that we've failed.

In reality, it's OK to just be OK. A helpful step in your self-love journey is to focus on accepting yourself as you are.

If you're thinking, *But Mary, I want to make more money, be a better mom/wife/sister/friend, and achieve more milestones in my life. If I accept where I am, won't that just make me complacent?*

To that I say hell no! The opposite is true. It's way easier to reach your goals, change your habits, and grow as a person when it comes from a place of acceptance rather than force.

you can't change what you don't accept.

You know what happens when you try to force your romantic partner to change: They don't! Unless they really want to change for themselves, they will never change for you. That's why you can't force yourself to change either. If you're truly committed to making a change in your life, the starting place is ALWAYS accepting where you are in this very moment. Even in drug rehabilitation programs, acceptance comes first. True and lasting change will never happen unless you can honestly acknowledge where you are now and love yourself anyway.

Hating yourself is exhausting. Loving yourself frees up your energy for what truly matters: you, your well-being, and having meaningful relationships with those you love.

So no, you won't get fat, lazy, and ugly if you start loving yourself. Quite the opposite!

side note: I use the word "fat" here because I know this is a concern for many, even though there is nothing wrong with existing in a larger body. We will address and dismantle this misguided belief later on in this book!

.... **is self–love the same as positive body image?** ....

Due to my lifelong struggle with body image issues and constantly wanting to change how I looked, I used to think that self-love was just about liking your body. I would see this reinforced on social media. I'm talking about those pictures of girls, usually with "perfect" bodies (read: thin, tanned, and toned), wearing a bikini on some dreamy beach, with captions like, "Love your body, because it's the only one you got!" I would think, *Wow, so that's what loving yourself looks like*. So why didn't it look like that for me? I've come to realize that true self-love has very little to do with positive body image. Sure, it's a part of it, but I like to think of self-love as a big pie that encompasses so much more.

THE SELF-LOVE PIE

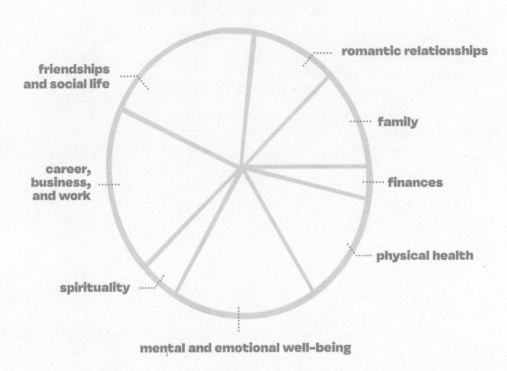

See? Body image doesn't even have its own category! Having a positive body image fits into both mental and emotional well-being and physical health, but it's only one piece of them.

If you're like me and you have a history of struggling with body image, it might seem like most of your self-love journey revolves around feeling comfortable in your skin. This is totally OK. I think body-image issues lead many people to this self-love journey, myself included. The most important thing is that you are here.

But what started out for me as a positive body-image journey turned into a lifelong self-love journey. I quickly learned that I got most of my self-esteem from other people's opinions. It didn't matter if it was receiving an award at school or catching a guy checking me out; the only time I felt good about myself was when I felt validated by other people—and usually people I didn't even care about! I realized that my obsession with having the "perfect body" stemmed from this obsession with "being perfect" and my overwhelming need to always keep myself, and everything around me, in control. This manifested into controlling my food, my grades, other people's opinions, and more. I realized that the root of all this was likely my tumultuous childhood, which led me to constantly finding myself in relationships that were equally turbulent, because I didn't know my worth. I thought I truly deserved the constant yelling and fighting, because, well, it's all I had ever known.

I'm sharing all of this to show you that I uncovered a lot more than issues with food, weight, and body image. Your self-love journey will ultimately open up so much more than you think. It's about getting to know yourself on such a deep level that you are conscious of everything you do, say, and even think. It's about changing your perspective to see your "imperfections" in a more positive light, just like my little sister taught us when she said, "It's not my fault I'm messy! I'm just creative!" With self-love, you open yourself up to more joy, more pleasure, and more opportunities, because you know you are worthy of good things—things that go way deeper than your appearance. You become free to simply be you, the woman who's always been there, waiting for you to love her.

where do you need more self-love?

The Self-Love Pie is a helpful tool, because it reminds you that you need self-love in all areas of your life. Depending on your situation, you might find that you long for self-love in some areas more than others, but this will also change based on what's going on in your life or simply the time of day.

For instance, if you're about to go into an important meeting at work, you might need to pump yourself up and tell yourself how great you are at your job, how much value you bring to the business and everyone in it, and how prepared you are for new challenges. But when you come home to your family, you might need to give yourself some compassion and reassure yourself that everyone will be just fine eating takeout for dinner so you can carve out some time for self-care. The focus of self-love varies day by day, hour by hour, season by season.

As I mentioned earlier, my self-love journey started because I wanted so desperately to feel comfortable in my body. I was so focused on body acceptance that it took me a while to realize there were other areas of my life that needed self-love too. The Self-Love Pie helps you consider different parts of your life and assess how you're feeling in each one. You may feel pretty comfortable with your body and your physical health but struggle when it comes to romantic relationships and finances. That's totally fine! But it's important to become aware of these patterns.

The Self-Love Pie is a holistic tool that can help you intentionally assess how you're feeling, acknowledge these feelings, and learn to love yourself completely. To illustrate, I'll share how self-love has improved each of these areas of my life.

1. romantic relationships:

As I touched on earlier, I used to date people who were verbally abusive. I remember my first boyfriend screaming at me outside my house after the homecoming dance. He was so loud that my mom heard him from her upstairs bedroom! This pattern kept repeating. Sadly, at least three guys I've seriously dated would regularly yell and scream insults at me. Once I started loving myself, I simply stopped letting people treat me that way. I had the awareness to recognize when I wasn't being treated right, the strength to stop associating with people like that, and the self-worth to know I deserved better.

2. family:

My whole family is from Russia, and in our culture, commenting on someone's weight or appearance the second you see them is totally normal and even perceived as necessary. Going to family dinners was stressful for me—especially as a disgruntled teen dealing with an eating disorder—in a family where "You've gained weight!" is a compliment when you're a kid but turns into an insult somewhere between adolescence and adulthood. Self-love taught me how to create boundaries, even if it meant telling my babushka (grandmother) that comments about my body were not welcome. After I started setting healthy boundaries, I noticed that I enjoyed family time more, because I wasn't always bitter and resentful.

3. friendships and social life:

Before my self-love journey, I based my social life around making sure other people liked me. It didn't matter if they were my longtime friends or I'd just met them; I needed to be liked by everyone in order to feel "OK." When I started liking myself, this need for approval naturally faded away. Now, I attract incredible people into my life who like me for who I am and who I don't feel I need to constantly please. My friendships are stronger, because I am no longer coming from a place of lack (e.g., "Please like me!") but from a place of genuine curiosity and connection.

4. career, business, and work:

This is a huge one for me. My entire career path has done a complete 180 since embracing my self-love journey. When I was competing in bikini fitness competitions, I was a personal trainer and thought I would work in the fitness industry for life. I was in school, studying business, so I figured maybe one day I'd have my own personal training business. When I finally decided to quit my destructive lifestyle and focus on healing instead, I knew my whole fitness career was shot and that I had to find something else. But I had no idea what that might be. Then, when I started sharing my self-love journey on social media, all these women spoke up and said, "OMG! I'm going through that too!" My social media blew up. I organically grew my coaching business online and then started speaking on stages and hosting worldwide self-love retreats. And now I'm writing this book for you! If I were still trapped in the cycle of self-hate, there's no way any of this would have happened.

5. finances:

Knowing your worth isn't just about relationships, but also about knowing you deserve to be compensated accordingly for your work and services. Studies show that women consistently undervalue themselves when it comes to asking for a raise—by a lot. According to Katty Kay and Claire Shipman's research in *The Confidence Code*, women ask for 30 percent less money than men do for the same job!

I see money as a form of energy, which means that getting paid for your work or services should be an equal exchange of energy. When I didn't value myself and therefore didn't value my work, I was OK with staying in a job that required a lot more out of me than I was being paid for. I didn't have the confidence to ask for a raise, nor did I really feel like I deserved one, because I was constantly undervaluing myself. Since I began this self-love journey, I've realized that I am worthy of making money, because it's a tool that allows me to feed my family, help people, and experience more in life. I started investing the money I made from my waitressing job in my coaching business, and even though making ends meet was tough for the first 3 years, eventually money started coming in, because I didn't give up. Self-love builds self-esteem, which empowers you to charge what you're worth, invest in yourself and let others invest in you, and make all the money you deserve.

6. physical health:

I used to think that being healthy meant going to the gym every day and eating salad (hold the dressing) for every meal. I would run on the treadmill for hours, exhausting my poor body, and then go lift weights for another hour. I thought the only way to achieve physical health was to have the perfect diet and exercise 7 days a week. Little did I know that that would actually destroy my health. It's been proved time and time again that going on a restrictive diet is not healthy and does not work in the long term. Now I know that health is not about what you eat or how much you work out; it's how you think and feel about yourself as a whole. Eating intuitively and listening to my body has made me feel healthier physically and also drastically improved my mental health.

7. mental and emotional well-being:

Self-love is ALL about how you feel about yourself on the inside. I never knew that mental health was part of my overall health, because I didn't grow up in a family where mental health was ever talked about. Looking back, I know that I struggled with an eating disorder through my teen years, even though I didn't see it back then. Self-love gave me the mental strength and emotional intelligence to accept where I was, overcome my eating disorder, and continue coaching myself through my struggles. Now, my mental and emotional health are as important to me as my physical health. I process my feelings as they come and do not let my negative thoughts consume me, because my self-awareness allows me to recognize them and address them with self-compassion instead of self-criticism.

8. spirituality:

Self-love has been quite the spiritual journey for me, from diving into Buddhist practices like meditation to simply feeling a connection with my bigger purpose on this planet. I was always a spiritual person, but self-love has deepened my capacity to love in general. Because I am kind to myself, I'm kinder to others. Because I'm more in tune with my needs, I'm more empathetic to the needs of others. Because I feel comfortable in my physical skin, I have the brain space to focus on the things that give my life purpose and meaning and feel a sense of connectedness to something greater than myself.

your own self-love pie

How do you envision self-love benefiting you in each of these areas?

1. romantic relationships:

_____
_____
_____
_____
_____

2. family:

_____
_____
_____
_____

3. friendships and social life:

_____

_____

_____

_____

_____

4. career, business, and work:

_____

_____

_____

_____

_____

5. finances:

_____

_____

_____

_____

_____

4. physical health:

_____

_____

_____

_____

_____

7. mental and emotional well-being:

_____
_____
_____
_____
_____

8. spirituality:

_____
_____
_____
_____
_____

DRAW YOUR OWN

SELF-LOVE PIE

do the thing!

Now that you have an idea of how self-love can help you in all these areas, pick one area you'd most like to work on right now and then decide on one thing you're going to do to address your needs and give yourself more love in this area. For example, if your chosen area is romantic relationships, then maybe you could challenge yourself to tell your partner about your self-love journey or strike up a conversation with a crush. Pick one action item and DO the thing! I promise you'll feel accomplished, self-assured, and empowered—and ready to do more.

which area of the Self-Love Pie are you choosing to focus on?

_____

_____

_____

_____

_____

what is one thing you are committed to doing to further your self-love in that area?

_____

_____

_____

_____

_____

I hope you see now that self-love isn't just about "feeling pretty" or taking bubble baths and using face masks. That certainly can be part of it sometimes, but it's about so ... much ... more.

chapter 3
rewriting your beliefs

rewriting your beliefs

When my mom was pregnant with me, she and my dad emigrated from Russia to the United States in search of a better life. Anti-Semitism was very present in Russia at the time, so the move came with relief and opportunities she wouldn't have had otherwise. However, it also came with new challenges: leaving friends and family back home, learning a totally new language, trying to find a job without speaking fluent English or having an American education, and adjusting to life in a new country. A couple of years later, my parents divorced, which was a long, nasty, and heartbreaking process.

There's no way to sugarcoat the fact that my parents' divorce messed me up. It tore me apart, sucked me dry.

And for so long, it made me believe I was unlovable.

It's not that I was actually unlovable. In fact, my parents fought for custody of me because each of them wanted me so badly. But I saw things differently. I felt and absorbed their fighting, their absence, and their separation. I thought that somehow it was my fault.

When you're a child, you're like a sponge. Every thought, every feeling, every emotion around you, you soak them all in and absorb them into your belief system. So at the young age of 3, I subconsciously started believing I was unlovable. That feeling was rooted within me before I was old enough to understand why I felt that way. But it became a part of me, and it led to a whole host of other issues to work through as a teen and young adult. I fell into abusive relationships with guys, because I didn't think I deserved anything better. I said yes too many times when I really wanted to say no. I spent my life trying to get other people to like me without ever questioning why I didn't like myself. I did all of this because, deep down, I believed I was unlovable.

As a child, your beliefs are pretty straightforward, because they're based on your observations about the world and how you learn to operate within it.

Lying helps me, because I get in trouble less when I lie.

If I were a better person, then I wouldn't get yelled at, blamed, or abandoned.

Fighting is normal, because my parents do that a lot.

As you grow into adolescence, though, these thousands of microbeliefs start to fit together like a puzzle and become your complex internal belief system, which informs what you believe about yourself.

If you get used to lying a lot, then you'll believe it's an effective tool and carry the habit with you.

If you're constantly being yelled at, put down, or rejected, then you'll believe that it's because you're not a good enough person.

If your parents were abusive to each other, then you'll believe that it's because abusive relationships are normal and will likely find yourself in a similar situation.

Belief systems become a huge part of your identity. Once solidified, you tend to protect your identity, even if it doesn't serve you. The trick is to remember that you are not born with these belief systems! You acquired them from your upbringing, subconsciously attaching meaning to every experience. Most of the time, you formed these beliefs as a way to protect yourself and find your place in this world. These beliefs may have helped you deal with certain challenges, struggles, or traumas, but they no longer have to run your life. You always have the power to step back and re-program these beliefs into ones that actually empower you.

truth or belief?

Just like your thoughts, your beliefs are not THE truth. They're just your truth. And they are unreliable, because they're based only on your personal outlook, not the whole picture.

This means that most of your negative beliefs are actually lies you tell yourself and internalize as the truth.

I know this is some heavy stuff, but I want you to look back at your childhood. Can you identify a difficult experience or relationship from your past that informs what you believe about yourself today? For instance, was there ever a time when you felt like something was your fault, even though you know now, as an adult, that it wasn't? Or did you want your parents' attention so badly that you bent over backward for their approval, validation, and love without knowing that real love is supposed to be unconditional? Or did someone you trust say something horrible to you that you've carried with you your whole life?

This shit affects you!

If you're going through life wondering why you have trust issues, you may have a belief system that says, "Everyone I trust ends up screwing me over."

If you're constantly dieting and feeling guilty about what you eat, perhaps you have a belief system that says, "If I'm not thin, I won't be attractive or loved." (Spoiler alert: Unfortunately, most women have this belief.)

And if you constantly find yourself in relationships with people who lie, cheat, yell, or don't treat you well in general, you could have a belief system that tells you you're not worthy of a healthy friendship/partnership/relationship, because you never had an example of that growing up. (This was a huge one for me.)

These are just a few examples, but you hold beliefs based on what you've observed and experienced in your life, and those beliefs often end up affecting your self-esteem, self-worth, and self-compassion, which affects your ability to love yourself. (Remember the Self-Love Formula?)

what you experienced
+
what you told yourself based on that experience
x
repeat 'X' number of times

=BELIEF ABOUT YOURSELF

all your beliefs added together = BELIEF SYSTEM

Luckily, your belief system is not set in stone. I came to realize that being a child of divorced parents also made me the independent, adaptable, and resilient woman I am today. But I only became empowered by this part of my story after I did the work to rewrite what I believed about the situation and, therefore, what I believed about myself.

You can do the same.

accept and forgive

Before you dig deep into your belief systems, you have to forgive yourself and others for the painful things that happened in your past. If you carry around heaviness associated with your past pain points and traumas and never take the time to fully process and release them, they will continue to hold you back.

For example, my curves used to cause me a tremendous amount of pain. They symbolized unwanted attention, failing to have the idealized thin body, and many stereotypes associated with being curvy—like guys expecting me to do certain things with them, being slut-shamed at school, and dealing with sexual harassment, among other things.

In 10th grade, I was sent to the office for violating the dress code, because I was wearing "short" shorts and a tank top with straps that were 1 millimeter smaller than the required two-finger width.

Even though the school claimed the dress code applied to everyone, I always felt like I was targeted more often because of my curvy body. In other words, the punishment wasn't about the length of my shorts but rather the curve of my butt. It wasn't about the width of the straps but the exposure of my well-developed breasts, which were seen as "distracting to boys" (in the wise words of the school administration).

Because I was held in the office, I was late to my biology class. After my (male) teacher pointed out to the whole class that I was late because of my outfit change—dress code "violators" had to change into dark green gym shorts and a gray gym T-shirt—he said, "Well, it doesn't surprise me that you got dress-coded. I mean, it's you."

I was so embarrassed and ashamed. What was that supposed to mean? Did my teacher just slut-shame me for the way I dressed? In front of the whole class? Did everyone think that about me?

And the worst part was that I couldn't do anything about it. His words weren't enough of a direct attack to take to the principal and, given all the snickers from my classmates, I didn't feel like I had the social support to stand up for myself.

Throughout my adolescence, I experienced all sorts of unwanted attention for my body, but the situation with the biology teacher stands out most vividly because it came from an adult, a teacher, an older man. After that incident, I became afraid of the attention and felt a strong desire to hide myself. This led to the grueling cycle of trying to make myself thinner, smaller, and more invisible.

I didn't want people to make assumptions about me like my biology teacher did.

I didn't want girls at school to call me a slut.

I didn't want boys to stare at me in that hungry way and assume I'd "do things" with them.

My struggle with body image and an eating disorder was my way of trying to deflect attention. It didn't matter if that attention was positive or negative.

Now, what I just shared with you took me a hot minute to realize. It's not like at 15, I was thinking, *I'm subconsciously associating my curves with unwanted attention, which is why I'm trying to make myself smaller both physically and metaphorically.*

No way! These kinds of insights took YEARS to realize, and I'm still discovering and uncovering the roots of my body-image pain. But once you can connect the dots of how you're subconsciously reflecting your emotional pain in your everyday life, you can begin to rewire those connections and heal your self-destructive thoughts and habits.

I shared this story to demonstrate that a lot of your pain does not necessarily come from dramatic, traumatic life events. Sometimes the little things can affect you more than the big things. Maybe it's a passing comment your mom made about the way you looked one day or a childhood best friend fading away because she decided your interests weren't "cool" anymore. No matter where it comes from or how minor it may feel, it's valid, it's real, and it needs to be healed and released.

Hear me when I say this:

your pain was NOT your fault, but the healing is your responsibility.

And the only way you experience healing is through forgiving.

Forgiving yourself.

Forgiving others.

Forgiving whatever defining experiences affect how you feel about yourself today.

Keep in mind that forgiveness doesn't mean you're making an excuse for someone else's wrongdoing. It means you're accepting what happened, letting go of the negativity that's eating you alive, and choosing a new future for yourself.

connect the dots

This next exercise can be emotionally charged, so take all the time you need. Make sure you're in a safe space, where you have the privacy to let your emotions flow. Don't hold back. Write out every ounce of feeling. There are no right or wrong answers. As you work through the prompts, go deep. Take time to think about your past experiences—even in early childhood—what beliefs they formed, and how they may still be affecting you. Close your eyes and identify where you are holding these painful beliefs or feelings in your body. This is not a surface-level exercise. You are peeling back the layers to uncover who you really are.

✦ **i am ashamed of ...**

_____

_____

_____

_____

✦ **this shame made me believe i ...**

_____

_____

_____

_____

✦ **i am angry at ...**

_____

_____

_____

_____

✦ **the reason for my anger is ...**

_____

_____

_____

✦ **i am afraid of ...**

_____

_____

_____

✦ **this fear comes from ...**

_____

_____

_____

✦ **i judge _____ for ...**

_____

_____

_____

✦ **i get jealous when ...**

_____

_____

_____

✦ **this jealousy makes me believe i ...**

_____
_____
_____
_____

✦ **the reason i judge others or myself so harshly is because i'm afraid that ...**

_____
_____
_____
_____

✦ **i feel pressured about ...**

_____
_____
_____
_____

✦ **this pressure comes from ...**

_____
_____
_____
_____

✦ **i feel resentful toward ...**

_____
_____
_____
_____

✦ **this resentment comes from ...**

_____

_____

_____

_____

✦ **i feel embarrassed when ...**

_____

_____

_____

_____

✦ **i'm scared that others will think ...**

_____

_____

_____

_____

✦ **this insecurity comes from ...**

_____

_____

_____

_____

I hope you felt a sense of relief as you unearthed so many deep thoughts, feelings, and emotions that have been bottled up inside. Know that these beliefs are a part of you, but they don't have to define you. After doing this exercise, it's important to give yourself some time to process and reflect on everything that's come up for you.

learning not to judge your thoughts

When you first start practicing self-awareness, you'll notice things about yourself that you never even knew were there. You'll start connecting the dots and figuring out why you are the way you are (read: why you think the way you think). And often, once you become aware of all these things going on inside your head, you'll want to quickly change them so that everything feels better right away.

But before you reframe what you believe about yourself, you have to accept what is. You know when you catch yourself feeling stressed out and you're like, *Ugh, I shouldn't be stressed, because stress is bad,* and then it makes you more stressed, because now you're stressed about being stressed?

I fell into this negative thought spiral quite a bit at the beginning of my self-love journey. When I caught myself feeling something negative, I would go into this spiral of resistance (Mary, you shouldn't be feeling this way.); forcefulness (Mary, just stop feeling this way.); guilt (Mary, I can't believe you preach self-compassion but now you're beating yourself up.); shame (Mary, you are seriously out of control.); impostor syndrome (Mary, if anyone finds out that you're feeling like this, they'll discredit you and never listen to anything you say.); hopelessness (Mary, you'll probably feel like this forever, because everything sucks, and it will always suck for you); and panic (Mary, oh my god, this feeling really will last forever, and you will never feel good again. What do we do?!) It's almost like after I identified my negative beliefs, I thought that I should be able to shift out of them right away. Then I beat myself up when I couldn't, and the whole cycle would start again!

But here's what you need to remember: Whatever you're feeling is OK. It's normal. And it's actually necessary. Judging, blaming, and shaming yourself for how you feel is counterproductive. Not to mention, these negative beliefs are formed from a lifetime of experiences! It's going to take some time to create new, more empowering beliefs in your head. I know it may not feel like it, but all the negative thoughts are trying to protect you from getting hurt. They're well intentioned but not conducive to your goal of unconditional self-love.

accept & release

Before you go into rewriting your beliefs, you must breathe through your feelings and accept what is. The way to do this is through awareness. Go back to the previous section and pick one belief to work with, and then:

1. Pause and breathe. Take a moment to simply notice what you're feeling about this belief without judgment.

2. Tell the negativity thank you, because it's simply a coping mechanism that's trying to keep you safe. For example, if your negative belief is, *My father left me, so why would anyone else stay with me?* Then tell that belief, "Thank you for trying to protect me from abandonment. I think I'm OK for right now." It feels counterintuitive, but once you accept the negativity, it'll no longer have power over you.

3. Ask yourself if this negative thought or belief is THE truth or just your truth? Is there a possibility that your negative belief is not true? Even allowing for the possibility of a different truth will help your brain look for more positivity.

This technique will allow you to shift from your head, where all those negative beliefs are running your life, to your heart, where unconditional self-love lives.

You can repeat this exercise with any negative thought or belief that comes up.

Now that you've accepted what is, I want you to do a releasing ritual for this toxic thought, feeling, or emotion. A release ritual is exactly what it sounds like: an action to symbolize letting go of an old, negative belief and creating space for something new, positive, and lovely.

Maybe you want to do a (safe) fire ritual, where you write down the belief and then burn that piece of paper. Or maybe you tear the page up into tiny shreds and then immediately throw away the pieces. Or maybe you call your best friend and ask them to join you in either of the above.

Whatever it may be, make sure to physically do something that represents accepting what's happened, letting it go, and becoming open to the new.

Your past no longer has to dictate how you feel about yourself. You are now free to form new beliefs and truths about yourself.

the power of your beliefs

When I first did the exercise of rewriting my old beliefs, I was feeling very stuck. I had just moved back home after a heart-wrenching breakup. I was struggling financially and hated relying on my parents for support. I didn't have any close friends, since I had recently moved back to Arizona and transferred schools. And I was studying full time at the university, which was not only kicking my butt but also making it difficult to work on growing my business. I just felt stuck.

Here's the exact new belief I wrote in my journal.

"I am continuously surrounded by women I LOVE who love, value, and appreciate me as much as I do them. The women who enroll in my online programs and who come to my retreats experience a positive transformation in their self-confidence and self-love."

To be clear, when I wrote this—in December 2018—I had never done a retreat, had no online programs, and did not feel like I was helping women at the level I wanted to.

It was simply a dream that I decided to make a belief. Instead of telling myself, *Oh, it would be nice...* or *I wish...*, or *One day I will...*, I decided to start living as though it were already happening.

And you won't believe how quickly it started happening for me. By March 2019, I hosted my first Self-Love Retreat in Sedona, Arizona, with 12 women who came from all over North America. My online following started growing exponentially, full of women on a self-love journey similar to mine. I met my two closest girlfriends and started dating someone who is supportive, caring, and loving! One year later, I signed the contract for the book you're reading now.

It's all possible. Everything you want is possible. It's just a matter of what you believe to be true about yourself.

···· **stepping out of the negativity bias** ····

If you're constantly telling yourself that you're not good enough, no one is going to love you, making money is hard, or everyone backstabs you, then of course your mind is going to be looking for proof of those things. Your mind doesn't care whether or not what you're thinking is true or healthy. Your mind just wants to say, "See, I told you so!"

Scientists call this concept a "cognitive bias," meaning your mind is biased toward what it's already thinking deep down inside. It's like when you call your friend for dating advice. If they say what you were already thinking (*Wait 10 minutes before you text back!*), then you're so much more likely to take that advice as proof that you were right in the first place. If your friend says something you don't agree with, then you'll probably ignore their advice and do whatever you already wanted to do.

So, your beliefs truly have the power to change your life. This process is about recognizing that for so long, you've been proving yourself right based on preexisting negative beliefs. Now it's about retraining your brain to prove yourself right based on new positive beliefs.

And it's OK if you don't subscribe to your new beliefs right away. You've been relying on your old beliefs for decades, so it's going to take more than reading a few pages of a book to permanently rewrite your beliefs in your head.

Your new beliefs should feel like a stretch and seemingly unfamiliar at first. The more you read them to yourself and feel all the emotions associated with them, the more real they'll start to feel and the more your life will change—for the better!

rewrite your beliefs

First, write down 5 negative things you believe to be true about yourself. I suggest referring back to the exercise on page 61 to see which beliefs have been in the back of your mind for a long time.

Then on the next page, rewrite those shitty, negative beliefs into new, more empowering ones. For example, the old belief I originally wrote down was, "People won't like me unless I'm thin (but not too thin); pretty (but not too pretty); and successful (but definitely not too successful!)." Then, I rewrote that old belief into this new one: "People who truly love me will always love me, no matter what I look like or how much money I make. They'll be genuinely happy for me as long as I'm happy."

The key is to make the new beliefs as detailed and specific as possible. The more positive feelings, energy, and emotions they have, the more real they'll feel.

When you're done creating your new beliefs, read them out loud to yourself. How do they feel? Do they make you feel empowered, excited, and emboldened? Good, that's the goal!

Now take your pen AND CROSS OUT THOSE SHITTY, OLD BELIEFS! From now on, they do not run your life because you have some new, self-lovin' beliefs to live by. If possible, tear out the page with your new beliefs and put it somewhere where you see it every day to remind yourself that you are worthy of these good things.

Take a picture of these pages. Look at them on your phone each day, or print them out and hang them somewhere you can see them. (I have mine on my bathroom mirror.) Read them to yourself every morning and every night.

old beliefs:

1. _____

_____

_____

_____

2. _____

_____

_____

_____

3. _____

_____

_____

_____

4. _____

_____

_____

_____

5. _____

_____

_____

_____

new beliefs:

1. _____

_____

_____

_____

2. _____

_____

_____

_____

_____

3. _____

_____

_____

_____

_____

4. _____

_____

_____

_____

_____

5. _____

_____

_____

_____

_____

chapter 4
self-love and other people

self-love and other people

Self-love is about putting yourself at the top of your priority list, living life on your own terms, and treating yourself as you would someone you love. But what happens when the people you love make it difficult? Whether it's family, friends, or your partner, other people's opinions can influence you and cause you to lose sight of your own. You can end up living in other people's heads instead of living in your own heart.

So I want to talk about how to love yourself enough to recognize when you're letting other people sit in the driver's seat of your life and learn how to take back the wheel. This chapter explores how to not let your family's opinions interfere with your life choices, how to stop people-pleasing your way through friendships, and how to keep your own identity when you're in a romantic relationship. You'll also learn about creating intimacy and setting bound-aries, because both are necessary elements of self-love.

what other people think

Caring about what I like to call OPO—other people's opinions—is what prevents you from pursuing a dance major in college and opting for something "safe" and "smart" like economics. (Well, maybe that was just me!) OPO can make you bend over backward and do things you don't want to do, just to avoid criticism. It can keep you from doing what you love, saying what you believe, and living life on your own terms.

I call OPO the sneaky, two-faced "friend," because sometimes she tricks you into thinking she is so important. I mean, what's wrong with wanting to please your parents and make sure your coworkers like you? But the more you start to care about OPO, she eventually comes back around to bite you in the ass, because if you constantly care what others think, then you'll find yourself living someone else's life, not your own. The price is way too high.

It's human nature to want to belong. Everyone wants to feel like they belong in their family, with their friends, and in society. Throughout ancient history, conforming to the status quo was how humans stayed safe. If you were exiled from the group, you were much more vulnerable to predators and could be in immediate danger. So, as a survival mechanism, evolution trained the brain to care about what others think so you wouldn't get shunned from the tribe.

These days, you don't really need approval from other people to survive. However, this mechanism in your brain still affects the choices you make, what you say and do, and how you act.

Things can get really out of hand when the pressure of OPO starts affecting your self-worth, making you feel like if you don't do what you're "supposed" to do, then you're not only temporarily shunned from the tribe but permanently kicked out, because you're not good enough to be in it. Sound familiar from the self-worth section?

And the worst part: You can internalize OPO so much that sometimes you think the expectations come from yourself. I remember when my therapist asked, "Who puts so much pressure on you?" And I said, "Nobody besides myself." To which my therapist replied, "Are you sure about that?"

I came to realize that my expectations of myself originated from a much bigger force: society's expectations of girls and women, which I so desperately wanted to meet. I internalized OPO so much that I didn't even realize what was driving my choices and was no longer in charge of my own life.

A study from the *Journal of Counseling Psychology* found that people who scored higher on a measure of authenticity (i.e., being true to yourself) had better self-esteem, more positive emotions, and greater happiness than those who scored low. This means that filtering out OPO and instead trusting your own internal compass is a huge part of loving yourself and living the life you want.

"should" talk

A big warning sign that you're living your life based on OPO is if you "should" on yourself. (Read that sentence out loud to hear the pun, which is very much intended!) Here are some common examples:

✦ i should be home by 5 p.m. to cook dinner, because if I'm not, then I'm not a good enough parent or partner.

✦ i should be married with two children, own a house, and have a steady job by 30, because if I'm not, then I'm not a good enough woman.

✦ i should get straight As in school, because if I don't, then it means I'm not smart enough to go to college or work the job of my dreams.

✦ i should save for a down payment on my house and shouldn't spend money on this vacation or retreat, because I don't really deserve them.

✦ i should be home by 5 p.m. to cook dinner, because if I'm not, then I'm not a good enough mom or wife.

✦ i should work overtime, because if I don't, then my boss won't think I'm a good enough employee.

Does any of this sound familiar?

Now you may read these statements and think, *What's wrong with cooking dinner for your family or saving up for a house?* Absolutely nothing ... unless you're only doing it because you feel like you should. The key distinction is the intention. If you're saving up for a house because you want to get a house, more power to you! I'm right there with you!

But if you're saving up for a house because your family expects you to or because you're scared your friends will judge you if you don't own a house by 30, then you're just living your life based on OPO.

And when you start deriving your self-worth from how many expectations you can meet, then you're in really big trouble, because guess what. It'll never be enough.

So how do you stop caring what other people think and let go of other people's expectations?

First, stop shoulding on yourself!

Anytime you catch the word "should" in your inner dialogue, question it, because it's a warning signal that you may be living based on OPO.

stop shoulding on yourself

write down one thing you feel like you should have, do, or be:

_____

_____

_____

who made you feel like you should?

_____

_____

_____

do you think this is an original thought, or a message you internalized from society?

_____

_____

_____

who are you afraid of disappointing?

_____

_____

_____

does their opinion really matter? will they stop loving you if you choose a route that's better for yourself?

_____

_____

is the negative consequence real or imagined? Would

_____

_____

what would be possible for you if you lived life on your own terms and did what you wanted to do?

_____

_____

✦

Now that you've worked through one of your shoulds, it's time to realize that all of these cultural expectations that affect you every day are made up! Think about it: Not so long ago, women were married off at 13 to a 45-year-old and expected to have three children by the time they turned 22. This isn't done anymore, because society has evolved and, therefore, changed the expectations of women. Who's to say that years from now, society won't look back and say, "Can you believe that people expected children to go $100,000 in debt to get a college degree in something they didn't really care about and then go into more debt to buy a house—and still pay thousands of dollars per month in mortgage payments for the next 30 years? And I can't believe women had to wear heels and pencil skirts! I mean, how impractical!"

I know I'm being sassy here, but I just want to give you a loving shake to wake you up a bit. So many of the expectations you place on yourself are just societal constructions. When you understand this, it's much easier to let that shit go. Visualize the courage you'll have when you live life on your own terms and not based on other people's opinions and expectations.

breathe in courage and breathe out other people's opinions.

As I wrote this book, sometimes I'd catch myself getting really caught up in OPO myself. *What if everyone hates this book? What if they think my writing isn't good enough?*

When I focused on other people's approval, I noticed that writing was a struggle. I dreaded the writing process and questioned every word I typed. I felt like my ideas weren't relevant enough and that my words weren't good enough.

When I caught myself feeling this way, though, I would go through my process of catching myself on my shoulds. I questioned why I felt this way and who I was trying to please. I would breathe in courage and breathe out other people's opinions.

I gave myself a few moments to work through the negative thoughts and embrace the fact that this book will resonate with the right people, and if it doesn't, at least I wrote it from a place of love and passion for the topic. As soon as I changed my mindset, writing became effortless. It began to pour out of me, because I was aligned with my inner guidance and stopped caring what my readers might think of it. (Of course, it's a bonus if you relate to what I'm saying, but it's not necessary in order for me to feel accomplished and fulfilled by the writing process).

At the end of the day, it doesn't matter what other people think of you. It matters what you think of yourself!

·············· **when the other people are your family** ··················

More often than not, the "other people" in your life are people you actually care about a lot: your family. You want them to approve of your choices. You don't want to burn bridges. And you want them to be proud of you. I mean, I get it. It feels good when your parents share your accomplishments on Facebook or when Grandma secretly admits that you are her favorite grandchild.

No matter where you come from or what your family situation is like, families tend to put you in boxes that dictate how you "should" be. Their opinions often influence how you choose to live your life, sometimes when you don't even realize it. Some of these expectations are influenced by your nationality, culture, or religion, while others come from the more nuanced aspects of your family dynamics.

Growing up, I received many conflicting ideas about girls and women and their role in society. Jaded by the divorce from my father, my mom raised me with the messages "Men only want one thing." … "Be careful who you get serious with." … "Don't rush into anything." … "Wait as long as possible to get married.".… "Get a good education, and find someone who is educated." … "Don't settle for anything less than you deserve." My dad, on the other hand, who is incredibly religious, always told me: "You're a girl, so you need to be nurturing, quiet, and polite." … "Get married as soon as possible." … "Respect your man." … "It's a woman's duty to bear children." My parents give me this conflicting advice to this day.

But I don't want to look back at my life and realize I made choices because I was trying to please my mother or my father. And I don't want to avoid marriage because I'm scared of it ending like my parents' did. I refuse to let their opinions and experiences stop me from living my life and making my own choices. I've been diligently working through all of this with a therapist to help me understand what I want when it comes to relationships, marriage, and family. I share this to show that it is totally normal to think about your family's opinions, but you can't let those opinions influence your actions.

The first step is to become aware that your family's opinions are affecting you. The easiest way to realize this is if you feel any kind of fear, stress, or anxiety when anticipating your family's reactions to your choices. Thoughts like:

◆   what if Dad gets mad when he finds out I switched my major?

◆   what will my mother-in-law think of my holiday dress?

◆   if I move out, will Mom be upset with me?

◆   will my family like my new boyfriend/girlfriend?

◆   what if they judge my choice to take a gap year and travel the world?

Sound familiar? When these fears come up, tell yourself, *My family wants the best for me, even if it doesn't seem like it sometimes. But at the end of the day, I am the only one who knows what is best for me. I am going to do what's best for me and trust that my family will come around.*

I want to emphasize that your parents and your family are not bad people, and they probably have good intentions. Your dad wanted the best for you when he told you that unless you studied hard, earned good grades, and landed a comfortable 9–5 job, there's no way you'd be successful. And your mom thought she was doing you a favor when she put you on a diet in middle school, because she was also brainwashed into thinking that diets are healthy and being skinny is important.

But at a certain point, you have to break free from the chains of OPO, even when they have good intentions, even when they may be "right," and even when they're coming from the people you love the most. You have to love yourself enough to stop letting other people's opinions replace your own.

your family's expectations

Take a moment to think about any expectations your family placed on you as you were growing up. Was there a certain way you were supposed to dress or look? A certain way you were supposed to act (sit up straight, cross your legs, don't be loud, be polite)? How did they see your gender and your sexuality? How did your family members speak of other people they didn't agree with? Were you pressured into a particular education or career path? Who did your family want you to be?

Now be honest with yourself as you answer the following questions.

~~~~~~~~~

some expectations my family placed on me were ...

_____

_____

_____

_____

_____

am i still trying to live up to these arbitrary family expectations?

_____

_____

i've been trying to live up to these expectations by ...

_____

_____

_____

_____

_____

_____

_____

_____

what would happen if i let go of these expectations? what would be possible for me?

_____

_____

_____

_____

_____

_____

_____

_____

Instead of trying to live someone else's life, choose to live your own life. Set boundaries with your family by expressing what is and is not OK (more on this later). Decrease the amount of time you spend with family members who don't accept you for who you are. Trust that those who love you want the best for you. But no one has the right to tell you how to live your life. It's up to you to be brave, express what you need, and live on your own terms.

··············· **when the other people are your friends** ···············

If you're anything like me, you like making people happy, especially your friends. Feeling down in the dumps? Let me spend an hour on the phone with you, giving you an inspirational speech. Need to vent about your significant other and dump all your emotions out on me? I'm here for it. Want to go out to the club? I'll go with you, even though I'm dead tired and have an early morning meeting. Bored on your day off? Come over and hang out, even though I'm supposed to work from home today, but I can catch up tomorrow, right?

We as people pleasers thrive off making our friends happy, because it gives us temporary relief and reassurance that we are liked, we are needed, and we belong. But have you ever felt like this intense desire to make your friends happy often comes at the expense of your own well-being?

Yeah, me too. But I've come to discover that true friendship doesn't leave you feeling drained and isn't one-sided.

The problem is that you often think you're being nice when you say yes when you really mean no or when you hold back from expressing your feelings at all, because somehow, other people's feelings seem more important than your own. But the truth is, by being nice, you're not always being kind, and kindness is the foundation of any true, meaningful relationship.

Being nice is defined as pleasing, agreeable, and delightful. Notice that this depends solely on how other people perceive you. Being kind, on the other hand, is defined as having, showing, or proceeding from benevolence, meaning it's all about your intention. If you just want other people to like you—even if it means not being the real you—then being nice will accomplish that. But if you want to be truly kind, then you have to stay true to yourself in the process.

I had a close friend in high school who was one of the nicest people on the planet. She was bubbly and sweet and wanted to make everyone around her happy. On the surface, it was hard not to like her, but her people-pleasing ended up hurting her and her closest friends, including me. Our weekend plans would often get canceled because so-and-so also asked her to hang out and, "They'd be mad if I said no." It felt like her life revolved around giving people rides, agreeing to everything, and being "friends" with everyone. She would often feel overwhelmed and have panic attacks, because having so many people rely on her was a lot of pressure.

Even though my high school friend wanted to be a good person, sometimes the friendship didn't feel genuine. I never knew if she was hanging out with me because she truly wanted to or because she didn't want to disappoint me. Maybe you have a friend like that, or maybe you are that friend. People-pleasing is common (especially among women and people who feel like they need to "earn" their worth), and it works for a while but eventually will become an issue in friendships. Once you approach friends from a place of self-love and kindness, instead of a frantic need to be liked, you'll naturally start to form healthy, genuine friendships with people who like the real you.

Here are some ways to stay true to yourself and not let OPOs influence you when it comes to friends:

- ✦ communicate your honest feelings
- ✦ stand up for what you believe in
- ✦ don't be afraid to say no
- ✦ stop apologizing for honoring your own needs
- ✦ make sure that when you say yes, you mean it
- ✦ only commit to plans you actually want to attend
- ✦ know that you don't always have to answer a text, pick up the phone, or respond right away
- ✦ separate yourself from other people's feelings and emotions
- ✦ set boundaries with your friends (see page 96)
- ✦ don't give too much of yourself unless there is reciprocity
- ✦ prioritize your well-being

If you feel exhausted from constantly trying to make other people happy, try making yourself happy first.

···················· **when friendships change** ····················

Have you ever heard of the crab mentality? If you've ever observed crabs in a bucket—you can find some entertaining videos online—there's always a determined crab that's passionately trying to make his way out of the bucket while the other crabs claw at him, literally bringing him down. This crab could easily escape the bucket, but the other crabs sabotage his efforts. It's like they're saying, "Haha, you want a better life for yourself outside of this bucket? Not on our watch!"

Crab mentality can undermine your growth as a human too. As much as you'd like to hope that most of your friends will be happy for your successes, sometimes the exact opposite happens. That's when you know that they're not true friends, because instead of giving you a lift to help you out of the bucket, they try to drag you back down through guilt ("Oh, you think you're better than us now?"); shame ("You're no fun anymore!"); and rejection ("I think we should stop being friends."). Some of your relationships, including your friendships, may change on your self-love journey. You may finally realize that you deserve better. Or as you get better at listening to your heart and speaking your mind, you may no longer agree to do things you don't want to, and some of your friends might not like that. Once you stop people-pleasing, some relationships will fizzle out, and that's OK, because those were never your true friends anyway.

Real friends will seek to understand you and ask how they can support you. Real friends will be inspired, rather than threatened, by your growth and success. Real friends will help you out of the bucket.

stay true to yourself

in friendships

do you think you may have people-pleasing tendencies?

○ *yes* ○ *no*

how have you been influenced by the opinions of your friends?

_____

_____

_____

_____

what are some things you do just to please your friends?

_____

_____

_____

_____

_____

do you have friendships that don't feel genuine? why?

_____

_____

_____

_____

_____

_____

what would happen if you stopped people-pleasing and started being true to yourself?

_____

_____

_____

_____

_____

_____

how would these friendships change?

_____

_____

_____

_____

_____

_____

which friends truly support your growth, success, and self-love?

_____
_____
_____
_____
_____
_____

how can you prioritize these friendships?

_____
_____
_____
_____
_____
_____

when the other people are
your romantic partners

I am a hopeful romantic. Yes, you read that right. The fantasies in my head of someone sweeping me off my feet and us falling in love and living happily ever after are filled with nothing but hope. While well intentioned and completely genuine, all hope about the future has caused me to cloud my perception of the present. More than once, I've given all of myself to the person I love, only to lose my identity in the process.

Does this sound at all familiar?

Of course when you're in love, you want nothing more than to make your partner happy and give them the best of yourself. But even though your partner's needs and input are important, they should never be more important than YOUR OWN.

Stop and read that again.

This means that if you're dreaming of starting a new business but afraid your partner would think it's crazy, do it anyway because YOU want to. If your friends are asking you to hang out Saturday but you don't know your partner's weekend plans yet, make the plans you want to have. If you want to wear that sexy outfit on your night out but your partner gives you a look of disapproval as you put it on, wear it anyway because it makes you feel good. Self-love is about being your own person, and this holds true even—or perhaps most of all—within your romantic relationships. You can't be your own person if you're constantly looking to your significant other for approval or living under their expectations.

As "me" becomes "we," make sure you still maintain your sense of self and do your own thing too. Relationships are about compromise, but you should never compromise so much of yourself that you lose touch with who you are, drift apart from your friends, or stop doing what you love. Remember: Even though your partner may be your "other half," you are still whole on your own. Self-love is a vital component of healthy romantic love.

let's talk about intimacy, baby

Intimacy is a deep connection with another person on an emotional, physical, or spiritual level (or multiple levels). Intimacy is deepened when you feel close to someone. Sometimes that happens when you're being sexual with your partner, and other times the most intimate moments happen when you're folding laundry together, going on a long car ride, or snuggling up on the couch.

When you're learning to love yourself, getting close to someone else can be challenging, because you're afraid they'll judge, criticize, and reject you the same way you tend to judge, criticize, and reject yourself.

But always having sex with the lights off and your T-shirt on because you're afraid they'll see your "flaws" will only make your body-image issues worse. Pretending everything is perfect and never sharing your insecurities will only make you feel disconnected. Refusing to trust someone and keeping your guard up will only make you feel isolated.

intimacy with someone else begins when you start accepting yourself.

And at the same time, being intimate with someone else can teach you self-acceptance. It's like a positive feedback loop: When you let someone in and it turns out OK, it makes you feel safer to do it again.

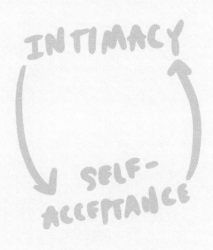

It's like when you have a horrible day and come home to your sweet dog greeting you with excitement and puppy kisses. Or when your children give you a hug when they see you crying. Or when your best friend gives you a pep talk. Or when your mom says, "I love you." Or when your partner gives you a long hug and a big kiss.

These are moments of intimacy that remind us we are worthy of love.

Sure, having more self-love deepens your ability to love others, but being more intimate with others can also teach you how to love yourself.

When I was struggling with an eating disorder, no one suspected anything, because I covered everything up with my glamorous bikini competitions and my commitment to fitness. Even my parents didn't know, because on the surface I was eating "healthy," being very active, and still excelling in school. I wouldn't let anyone in on my mental health struggle. I was afraid that no one would take it seriously, because I never took it seriously.

One day, after winning my second bikini fitness competition, my mom texted me and asked to meet for coffee. As I was driving to meet her, she sent me another text that said, "Sitting outside. I got you a mocha."

I absolutely FREAKED out at the fact that she got me a mocha. The calories. The sugar. The dairy. How could she?! Didn't she know I was on a diet?!

I ended up lashing out at my mom and ditching our coffee date before it even started. I drove away feeling so ashamed, because I couldn't believe I lost it on her like that. I went from being angry at my mom for getting me a mocha to being angry at myself for letting things get this far.

And at that rock-bottom moment, my mom sent me a text: "I just want you to know that I love you very much. And I am here for you anytime you need me."

My mom loved me when I couldn't love myself.

Even though this emotional breakdown probably wasn't the best way to open up to my mom about my struggles, it instantly made us closer. She realized I was dealing with something serious, and I realized she was there for me no matter what. From then on, she has been my biggest support system in healing.

I also remember the first time I had sex with the lights on. I was so nervous. I had gained some weight, and I was afraid that if my partner saw my body in full light, he wouldn't think I was attractive. But I pushed myself to try it. I wish I could tell you this romantic story about how he reacted to seeing my bare body, but I honestly have nothing to tell you, because guess what?

He didn't react. It was just … normal. He loved my body as much as always—cellulite, tummy rolls, and imperfections included. Even though it was a big deal to me, his lack of reaction made us closer, because I realized he loves me for me, not for my body.

And if someone shows signs that they only value your body, then they don't deserve to be intimate with you on any level!

Our journey to self-love is dependent on other people, not because we need their opinions to validate our worth, but because we need our loved ones, the people we trust most, to reassure us that it's OK to be our true selves and show us that love is unconditional.

because it is.

stay true
to yourself

in relationships

Reflect on the following questions to determine how true to yourself you remain in romantic relationships. If you see room for improvement, that's OK! That's what the self-love journey is all about: starting where you are.

who are you without your partner? describe your interests, values, and personality.

_____

_____

_____

_____

_____

_____

_____

_____

_____

_____

_____

_____

_____

_____

what are some things you like to do without your partner? list any hobbies, passions, or little acts of self-love you like to do by yourself.

_____
_____
_____
_____
_____
_____
_____
_____
_____
_____

describe a time when you were intimate with someone and that deep connection helped you feel more self-acceptance.

_____
_____
_____
_____
_____
_____
_____
_____
_____
_____

setting boundaries

For unconditional love to also be healthy, stable, and respectful, you need to learn to set boundaries in your relationships.

Sometimes it's easy to just stop hanging out with a friend who isn't supportive of you, but creating a separation often feels a lot more complicated. If you're anything like me, you're loyal to those you care about. Sometimes you're even loyal to a fault, sacrificing yourself to maintain a relationship with your family members and old friends. But there's a fine line between loyalty and self-sacrifice.

And that fine line is called a "boundary." Boundaries separate your needs, feelings, requests, and responsibilities from those of others. Correctly placed boundaries communicate how you allow others to treat you, how much you are able to give to others, and what is and is not acceptable in your space. Boundaries are important in all aspects of life, including friendships, family, romantic relationships, and the workplace.

For example, if your mom keeps calling you during work hours, even when you told her not to call unless it's an emergency, then you need to set a boundary so she stops interrupting your work time. If your friend keeps talking about her diet and you're sick of hearing about it, but she won't stop, then you need to set a boundary around this or else she'll keep bulldozing your conversations with diet talk. If you feel your boss is taking advantage of you by texting work-related matters to your personal cell phone, then you need to set communication boundaries or they'll keep invading your personal life.

The hardest boundaries to set and enforce are with the people most important to you, but they are the most necessary! Remember that setting boundaries is an act of love, because it's in support of the relationship. A boundary basically says, "Hey, I really want to nurture a healthy relationship with you, and here's what's going to help us do that."

And you don't have to wait until things are "bad" to set healthy boundaries in your relationships. That's like waiting until you're sick to take your vitamins! We all know vitamins are most effective when you take them consistently and proactively, and they don't do much when you've already caught a cold. Boundaries are the same way. They can save a tense relationship or make a good relationship thrive.

This is not about cutting people out of your life or being cold and rude. This is about being kind yet assertive. Healthy boundaries come from a good place and are necessary for your self-love journey.

Here's a five-step process for setting effective boundaries.

✦

1. ask for permission.

Remember, unsolicited feedback is rarely effective. If you come out and say, "Um, can you stop saying that shit?! It's really freakin' annoying!" the other person probably won't receive it too well. I start by saying "Hey, best friend, can I ask something of you?" or "Can I share some honest feedback with you?" Wait for them to give you the go-ahead before continuing. This also gives them an opportunity to say, "Hey, now's really not a good time. Maybe we can talk tomorrow?" That's their boundary, and it's your job to respect it. When people feel seen, heard, and acknowledged from the beginning, they're much more likely to listen to you and a lot less likely to get defensive. Asking for permission is a good communication tool for ANY situation.

2. communicate only how you personally feel.

Setting a boundary is something that's done for you, by you. Therefore, this is not the time to preach your opinions on what they should do (no one likes being "should on," remember?) but rather to express how you feel.

Remember that you experience everything through your own lens of interpretation, and someone else could have a totally different experience of the exact same situation. If you blame them, then they'll defend themselves. Instead, talk only about your own experience.

This is where those clichéd "I statements" come into play. Start every phrase with, "I feel …" instead of, "You make me feel …"

instead of...	*say...*
"You are acting this way ..."	"My experience is ..."
"You make me feel ..."	"I feel ..."
"I hate when you ..."	"It hurts me when you ..."

3. make a powerful request.

Now that you've asked for permission and expressed how you genuinely feel, it's time to make your powerful request, i.e., set your boundary.

When you communicate your boundary, keep the same intention as you had in #1: You are working together to nurture the relationship and make it better for both of you. And use the same I statements from #2 as much as possible so you don't come across as blaming the other person.

instead of...	*say...*
"Could you stop ..."	"I ask that you ..."
"Maybe you could ..."	"My request is that ..."
"You should ..."	"Can you do that for me?"

Stand in your power, and communicate your request clearly. Then, phrase the question so they're forced to give you a yes or no response to your request.

Here are the exact words I used with my friend who kept criticizing her body and engaging in diet talk around me: "My request moving forward is that we don't talk about our bodies anymore. I'm on a self-love journey and would like to only speak kindly about ourselves. Can you do that for me?"

Usually, ending with a question will make their response more positive, because again, they'll feel like they're an important part of the conversation.

If you want your boss to stop taking advantage of you or texting you on your personal phone, you can say something like, "I ask that work-related matters be sent to my email, because this would help me stay more organized. Can we agree to do that?"

You can be firm yet polite. You can be assertive yet kind. You can stick up for yourself without putting anyone else down.

The common misconception is that boundaries will make people not like you, but this couldn't be further from the truth. People appreciate clear communication. People are relieved when they know exactly what you need from them. People will respect you more when you set boundaries.

4. make sure they respond.

I'm sure you've been in a position where it felt like no matter how many times you said something, the other person didn't seem to hear you. This is why it's important to get some sort of answer or acknowledgment from the person with whom you're setting boundaries. A simple, "Sure, I can do that" or, "OK" can go a long way, because now it's not just a boundary you requested but one they agreed to. If someone ignores your boundary request, you may want to reevaluate the relationship.

5. hold them accountable.

It is your responsibility to make sure others honor your boundary. If someone violates your boundary and you don't hold them accountable, then the boundary will be lost. Remember, your close ones are humans, too, so don't expect them to be perfect, especially not right away. Instead, practice patience, remind them of your boundary, and follow through on consequences as needed.

The consequence doesn't always have to be something big like cutting the person out of your life. It can simply be refraining from discussing certain topics with that person, spending less time with them, or taking time and space for yourself to reground, regroup, and remind yourself that your feelings are valid.

Pay attention to how someone treats your boundary and the effort they put forth to fulfill it. If someone is stepping over your boundary over and over again, it's up to you to decide whether or not you want to keep that person in your life. At that point, you did everything you could. Sometimes the most effective boundary is walking away.

SELF-LOVE CHALLENGE
set a boundary

Using the steps on the previous pages, think of one boundary you can set with someone in your life. It doesn't have to be anything big, but think of something that has been weighing on you lately. Are you spending too much time or energy on someone who's not reciprocating? Set a boundary to limit your effort. Is there someone who keeps trying to take advantage of you? Set a boundary to not let it happen again. Do the people in your circle continuously make insensitive comments you don't agree with? Set a boundary to not discuss those topics anymore. Setting boundaries is about loving and respecting yourself even when you risk disappointing others.

part two

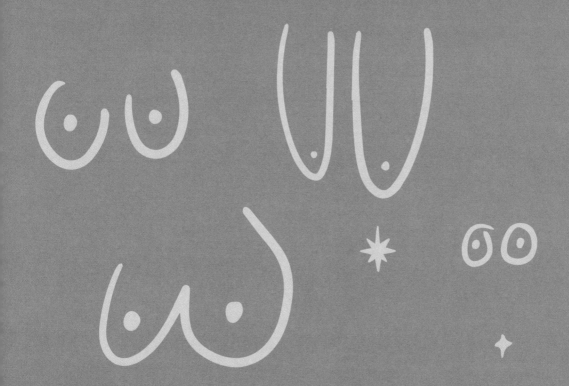

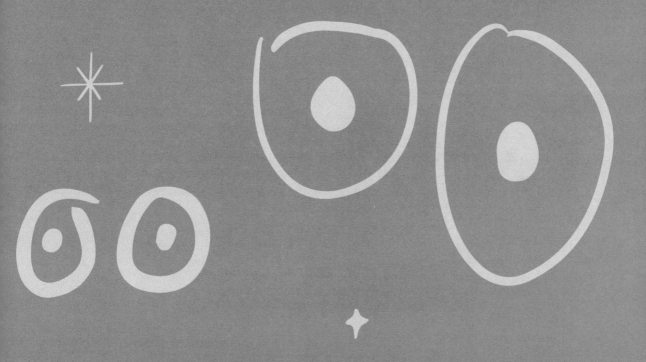

loving your body

chapter 5
the body-image trap

the body-image trap

Have you ever wondered how people felt about their bodies before there were mirrors, photographs, or social media?

I bet they weren't as worried about what their bodies looked like, because all they knew was how their bodies felt. Photographs came in 1826, and mirrors were invented in 1835. Before then, people didn't have the opportunity to look at themselves as much as we do now, so I doubt they were as stressed out about dimples, pimples, cellulite, or fat rolls! Today, especially with social media being omnipresent, you see your body (and other people's bodies) so often as an image that you forget that your body is an experience. You can become overly concerned with how your body looks rather than how it feels.

BODY EXPERIENCE > BODY IMAGE

Remember how I mentioned in the first chapter that my body-image issues were rooted in my craving for validation and acceptance? This is why it's important to take some time on your self-love journey to assess how you feel about your body, and how those feelings influence your perception of yourself as a whole. It is all intertwined.

In her book *Beauty Sick*, Dr. Renee Engeln presents some sad, but not surprising, statistics about women and body image. Eighty-five to 90 percent of surgical and nonsurgical cosmetic procedures are done on women. Nine out of 10 young people suffering from anorexia or bulimia are female. The World Health Organization surveyed over 200,000 young people in 42 different countries and found that among 15-year-olds, girls were more likely than boys to report that they were "too fat." Ironically enough, boys were more likely to be "overweight" than girls. (I don't necessarily believe in this language for defining weight categories, but for simplicity's sake, I'm using the wording from the WHO's report here.)

One of my Instagram followers recently sent me a video that made me cry. Her 9-year-old cousin made a TikTok video of herself doing push-ups. The caption said: "Doing these until I lose weight." At 9 ... years ... old. And by no means was she "chubby." Most people would see her as an average-size girl. You may feel sad right now, because no 9-year-old should have to worry about her weight. Or maybe you were her at that age.

I won't bog you down with more statistics, but there's plenty of research you can dig into about how dieting harms your health, especially during prime developmental years such as childhood and puberty. The numbers behind eating disorders are scary in every way, including how many people they affect, how quickly and secretly they develop, and how they can increase the likelihood of other mental health concerns, such as substance abuse, low self-esteem, anxiety, and other psychiatric disorders.

And even if you're not an extreme dieter or have never struggled with an eating disorder, it's nearly impossible to escape the sociocultural pressures to have a slim and fit figure. These beauty standards follow us everywhere, whether we're conscious of them or not.

How you feel about your body affects how you feel about yourself. While living in an image-driven society doesn't help the cause, what you can do is build up your own body confidence and inspire others to do the same. The more you do this, the more girls, women, and people everywhere will begin to see the body for what it is: a vessel that allows you to experience and LOVE yourself and your life.

your body is not an image. it's an experience. a beautiful experience!

the vicious body-image cycle

Have you ever woken up bloated in the morning, looked in the mirror, and felt bad about yourself? Or walked by your reflection in a window and hated what you saw? Or seen yourself in a photo and thought, *Damn, does my arm really look that big? I need to do something about that.* I think everyone has experienced some version of this thinking. Those thoughts are a bummer in the moment, but it's also important to consider the cumulative effect. When put together, all those "little" negative thoughts can end up seriously affecting your mood, actions, and interactions with others.

Maybe you have a negative body-image thought and then decide to punish yourself by skipping breakfast, wearing a big T-shirt instead of your favorite dress, and spend all day thinking about how much you hate your body.

To top it all off, you avoid striking up a conversation with the cute new barista at the coffee shop because you don't think you look good enough. So you spend the rest of the day feeling insecure, isolated, and incapable, all because of that one negative body-image thought you had in the morning. You call it a "bad day" and decide to start "fresh" (i.e. start a diet) tomorrow.

If you are really honest with yourself, how often do your "bad days" (e.g., a not-so-good moment that dictated your mood for the rest of your day) relate back to your body image?

When I was struggling with my bulimia, I went through this negative cycle ALL THE TIME. I'd wake up, "body check" myself in the mirror, and, if I looked the slightest bit bloated or "not skinny enough," I'd let that influence my mood, actions, and energy for the entire day.

Not only that, but I'd think, *Screw it! Since I feel like shit, I might as well look like shit too.* I'd put on an old, baggy T-shirt, tie my hair up into something that resembled a coughed-up fur ball, and run out the door, wearing the remains of yesterday's makeup.

And, of course, I'd feel really insecure and antisocial, because I did not take care of myself. I'd feel ashamed of how I looked, so I'd isolate myself as much as possible. Basically, I'd tell myself that if I didn't feel good in my body, I shouldn't feel good AT ALL.

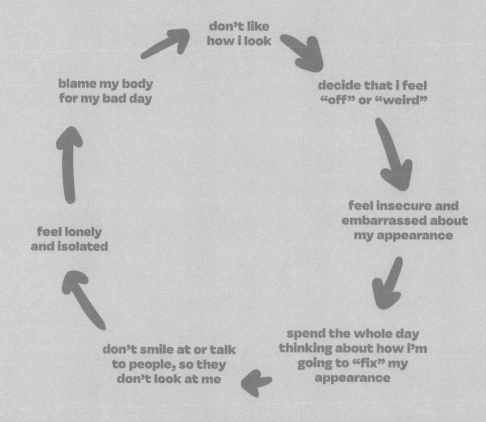

The biggest problem with this cycle is that I believed how I looked mattered. To me, looking "good" was a prerequisite to being happy. If I didn't feel like I looked good, I literally wouldn't let myself do things I usually loved doing. For example:

✦ i wouldn't strike up a conversation the person sitting next to me in class, because I didn't want them to look at me and judge my appearance.

✦ i wouldn't try to be friendly with customers at my restaurant job, because my mind was consumed by thoughts of how to burn off all those excess calories.

✦ i wouldn't go out on a date if I wasn't confident in my appearance. I decided to reject myself before anyone else could reject me.

why do i care so much about how i look?

Unfortunately, most women are raised to believe that how you look matters. Advertisements in the media don't just tell you to "lose weight," they tell you to lose weight so you can get the guy, feel confident, have friends, and be happy. If you've ever taken a marketing class or simply paid attention to how marketing messages are framed, they are always attached to an emotional outcome. So when Vogue puts Cameron Diaz on the cover of their "Ageless Style" issue and reveals her secrets to "20 years of beauty and power," then your consumer mind is programmed to associate beauty with power.

Not-so-fun fact: Research done by SkinStore, a beauty retailer, has estimated that the average "worth" of a woman's face in the U.S. is $8 per day, meaning women use $8 worth of skin care and cosmetics every single day. Women in New York spend an average of $11 per day on their faces, which adds up to nearly $300,000 in a lifetime! From morning cleansers, eye creams, and serums to foundation, mascara, and glossy lipstick, most of us spend a shit ton on our faces. And that doesn't include any other beauty routines!

The diet industry is worth over $72 BILLION in the United States (as of 2019). The beauty industry is estimated to be worth $532 billion globally and expected to reach a market value of $805.61 billion by 2023. Yes, this means that people worldwide will be spending almost $1 TRILLION on trying to look thinner, slimmer, younger, fitter, curvier, tanner, skinnier, sexier, and whatever else society adds to the list of things we need to change about our bodies.

Now remember that harmful marketing messages have infiltrated your mind for decades. From before you were born, your parents might have anticipated a girl … and purchased the pretty pink bows and cute dresses to go along with what society deems "cute." Basically, you were told to look a certain way before you were even born!

When you were a child, you probably observed the women in your family spending hours getting ready for a night out while the men, well, they looked how they always looked. Then, when you went to school and learned how to read, you started understanding that there were certain ways a woman "should" look to be more accepted in society. And don't even get me started on being a teenage girl, growing up with what seems to be a never-ending voice screaming, "YOUR LOOKS MATTER!" Boys rating girls, girls worrying if they look fat, parents paying for beauty services, from simple haircuts and highlights to waxing or laser hair removal. High school girls trying to look hot even in gym class—usually to attract boys and be seen as the pretty, popular girl—while the dress code tries to ensure they don't look "too sexy"—to not distract the boys, of course. And then there are the exorbitantly priced prom and homecoming dresses ... and the professional hair, makeup, and photographers to go along with them.

But it doesn't end there. College girls are pressured to look a certain way in class, impress everyone with their party outfit (which will also be posted on social media), and prioritize having a slim, fit body over studying for an exam or doing their homework.

I participated in all of the above, plus more.

The constant scrutiny of your appearance does not lessen with age. As you get older, you're expected to change the way you dress to more conservative styles (but not too modest, because you still have to keep up with the trends), hide your gray hairs, resist smile lines and wrinkles, and, oh yeah, lose the baby weight as fast as humanly possible. And if you don't, then you're blamed and shamed for "not taking care of yourself," "falling off the wagon," and not "bouncing back."

Women everywhere, from Hollywood to politics, are demeaned (read: bullied) for "looking old" and gaining weight, while men with gray hair "age gracefully," and society sees their "salt and pepper" beard as a sign of wisdom. No one bats an eye when a man carries some extra weight or has wrinkles—and it would NEVER make him vulnerable to public scrutiny or compromise his career opportunities.

On the flip side, women are rewarded, through praise, validation, and attention, for successfully adhering to society's beauty expectations. A prime example is how much Adele, the award-winning British singer and songwriter, was praised for her weight loss in 2020, even though she herself has said nothing about this weight loss. Adele is now a "before and after" picture, without having any say in the matter. This shows that even a woman who has achieved extraordinary accomplishments in her career is still being reduced down to her appearance, as if that's the most interesting and important thing about her.

When women are criticized for not abiding by society's beauty expectations and then praised for adhering to them, we all suffer from the message that our appearance matters a lot.

When I was preparing for my TEDx talk about body image, I practiced my speech in front of my public-speaking group. On my feedback form, one man wrote, "Next time, don't wear such baggy clothes. Your speech is about body image, so you should show more of your body." I was livid. A 50-something-year-old man disregarded everything I had shared in my speech and instead opted to comment on my looks. I couldn't help but think that if I were a man, nobody would care about what I was wearing or how I looked.

According to a survey by Fairygodboss that was featured on Forbes, hiring professionals most frequently said they'd hire a young, thin, Caucasian brunette. Out of 15 job candidates, the survey respondents reported that the oldest candidate seemed to have the three traits hiring professionals listed as most important when hiring: professionalism, leadership material, and reliability. But despite her high rankings, only 29 percent of survey respondents said they'd hire the older woman. Additionally, only 15.6 percent of hiring managers said they would hire an overweight woman. In fact, 20 percent described an overweight candidate as lazy, 21 percent described her as unprofessional, and only 18 percent said she had leadership potential. What's more, only 15 percent said they'd hire a female who frowns. When have you ever heard of a man being told, "Smile, sweetheart"?!

And the above study doesn't even scrape the surface of what life is like for women of color. In her book *So You Want to Talk About Race*, Ijeoma Oluo highlights that not only do white women earn 82 cents for every dollar a white man makes, but black women earn only 65 cents for the same job. Hispanic women earn even less: 58 cents for every dollar a white man earns. And that's assuming a woman of color is even hired in the first place, especially since studies show that if you have a "black sounding" name, you are four times less likely to be called for a job interview. Even though this is a deeper issue of systemic racism and sexism, it shows that the world values your outward appearance over the objective value you bring.

Does all of this make you angry? Good. It should.

It makes me very angry that those kinds of injustices against women exist in the world. It's sad that women are trained to believe that appearance matters so much. It's even more unfortunate that in some cases, it does. Even though you can't change racism, sexism, and deeply ingrained beliefs in society overnight, it's still up to you to untangle these toxic messages about beauty so you can learn to love yourself beyond your body.

SELF-LOVE CHALLENGE

tone it down

One thing you can do for yourself is become conscious of how much time, energy, and money you spend on fixing or maintaining your looks. Think about how much money you spend on beauty products and services (new clothes; the latest and greatest makeup products, skin care products, and facial services; hair products, haircuts, and hair removal with waxing or lasers; manicures and pedicures; and so on) and how many hours you spend on your appearance (getting ready in the morning, Googling antiaging hacks, shaving, looking at beauty influencers on social media, thinking about how you look, blow-drying your hair for eternity, etc.). Now take a moment to consider who all of this work is for.

is it genuinely for yourself?

Is it necessary every single day or only some days? Can you identify one or two ways you can cut down your routine and focus your energy, time, and money on something other than your appearance? Even if you try to merely *think* less about how you look, it's a step in the right direction. Remember, you do not owe the world any particular standard of beauty. Your only job is to show up as you.

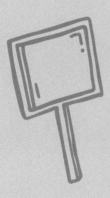

list 3 ways you will tone down your focus on your appearance:

1. ....
....
....
....
....
....

2. ....
....
....
....
....
....

3. ....
....
....
....
....

actions over feelings

Listen, your thoughts about your body are just that: thoughts, not facts. But thoughts create feelings, and feelings create your overall attitude about your body.

thoughts

feelings

overall attitude
about your body

One of the problems here is that your mind is predisposed to negativity. Think about it: When someone compliments you, it feels good in the moment, but you probably don't continue thinking about the compliment for the rest of the day. But when someone insults you, you might dwell on it for hours or days, if not months or years!

It takes effort, but you can heal your body-image struggles by not giving so much importance to negative thoughts in the first place. The only way to do this is to continue living your life even when you feel insecure about your appearance. As soon as you freak out about the negative thoughts in your head, they will have more influence over you.

Instead of falling into that pattern, try saying to yourself, "Hmmm, that's an interesting thought," and then moving on with your day. Do all the amazing things you wanted to do in the first place, and don't let those negative thoughts dictate your actions.

Basically, do not let your body image control your life EXPERIENCE.

Maybe you can go out in sweatpants and a messy bun, but instead of feeling insecure about your appearance and avoiding people, you go out of your way to talk to them anyway.

Or maybe instead of hiding your bloated belly behind baggy clothes, you wear your favorite outfit as planned.

Or maybe you challenge yourself to spend less time doing your hair and putting on makeup because there is absolutely nothing wrong with your natural look.

These kinds of actions will help reinforce the fact that you can still live a happy, fulfilling, and empowered life no matter what you look like or how you feel about what you look like. Practice having a good day EVEN IF you don't (yet) feel good about your body.

do not let your body image control your life EXPERIENCE.

That's my challenge for you this week: Next time you have bad body-image thoughts and feel tempted to let them ruin your day, open up this book, write them down, and then keep moving on with your day. (You might want to bookmark or put a sticky note on this page!)

keep moving

my three most prominent bad body-image thoughts:

1. ....

....

....

2. ....

....

....

3. ....

....

....

things i'm going to do, see, feel, and experience DESPITE those thoughts:

1. ....

....

....

2. ....

....

....

3. ....

....

....

Now, what would happen if you started looking at yourself less but feeling yourself more? Let's find out.

body neutrality

You've probably seen the term "body positivity" floating around on social media. It isn't bad to feel good about how you look, but I don't think body positivity is the answer. Changing your focus from hating your body to loving your body seems like a step forward but is still incredibly focused on your image. This attention on how you feel about your body—negative or positive—still keeps you obsessed with your thoughts about your body!

side note: "Body Positivity" comes from the political Fat Acceptance movement that was originally created in the 1960s. Fat acceptance is about ending the culture of shaming and discriminating against people based on their size, shape, weight, ability, or appearance. More recently, however, "body positivity" has gained popularity on social media as a way to help people feel better about their bodies, which seems to have pushed out the very people who created it (women of color, women with disability, and trans people).

It's great that more people are starting to appreciate their bodies, but we must give credit where it's due and acknowledge the true origins of this movement and include every BODY in it.

I don't know about you, but I don't want to be worrying constantly about feeling positively about my body. I just want to be. Plus, the pressure of always having to feel positive about your body can feel daunting, intimidating, or impossible. The last thing you want is to make this self-love journey feel like another thing you have to do perfectly and constantly.

So, instead of focusing on body positivity, I invite you to shift your focus to body neutrality—simply feeling neutral about your body. Body neutrality will help you see yourself as more than a body.

Because, well, you are so much more than a body.

more than a body

Here are some questions to help ease you into a body-neutral mindset.

~~~~~~

if you were trapped on a deserted island with no people, no mirrors, and no way to see your own reflection, how would you live your life?

_____
_____
_____
_____
_____
_____
_____
_____
_____
_____
_____
_____
_____
_____
_____

if scales, mirrors, and other people's opinions didn't exist, how would you feel about your body? would you even think about it that much?

think of your favorite memory from the past 5 years. describe that memory in detail.

_____

_____

_____

_____

_____

_____

_____

_____

_____

_____

_____

_____

_____

did your weight, size, or appearance have anything to do with the memory you described above?

○ *yes* ○ *no*

even if you don't love your body right now, what are three things you appreciate about it?

1. _____
_____
_____
_____
_____

2. _____
_____
_____
_____
_____

3. _____
_____
_____
_____
_____

chapter 6
reconnecting with your body

reconnecting with your body

Have you ever stood barefoot on the beach, feeling the cool breeze in your hair and the salty sea air on your skin, looking out at the ocean and experiencing a deep sense of calm and peace? Or sat in the forest, inhaling the smell of fresh pine, and knowing that everything will be OK?

We often feel most grounded when we're connected to nature.

But it's easy to forget that your body is a part of nature. You can feel this same sense of peace at any time, simply by connecting more deeply to your body.

Now that you have new ways to think about your body, it's time to explore ways you can reconnect with your body, such as experiencing pleasure, eating intuitively, moving through your feelings, and finding true health.

experiencing pleasure

Pleasure.

What comes to mind when you read that word?

Whisper it out loud to yourself.

Pleasure.

Pleasure is an all-encompassing moment when you feel good physically, emotionally, and spiritually. And no, pleasure isn't just about sex (although that's one way to experience it).

Think about having that first sip of coffee in the morning, hearing a baby giggle, smelling your favorite candle, or getting lost in a novel. These are all simple ways to experience pleasure.

One of the saddest things my 10-year battle with an eating disorder took away from me was feeling worthy of pleasure. I had convinced myself that food didn't taste good (because it has calories), sleeping in was unnecessary (because fasted cardio must be done at 5 a.m.), and I wasn't worthy of sexual pleasure (because I had to get rid of my cellulite before anyone could see me naked).

I was so consumed by thinking about food, worrying about how I looked, and exhausting myself with exercise that there was no room left to experience the simple pleasures of life—or feel very much at all.

If you think you're not worthy of pleasure until you lose X pounds, make X dollars, or have X thing, then hear me when I say this:

X pounds, X dollars, or X thing will not bring you pleasure. Your body is what allows you to experience pleasure. So if you're disconnected from your body because you see it as a thing to control, master, starve, contort, and exhaust into some perfect image in your head, you will also be disconnected from pleasure.

The body is the vessel that allows you to experience simple pleasures: dancing in your underwear while getting ready, kissing your loved ones, running full speed into the ocean, laughing until you can't breathe, playing tag with your children, walking in nature, having earth-shattering orgasms, breathing deeply in moments of stress, traveling to exciting new places, and more.

A big part of reconnecting with your body is allowing yourself to experience pleasure as much as possible. The more you do this, the more you will love all that your body allows you to experience.

So curl up and read that romance novel. Pause when you feel that first sip of coffee hit your lips. Do that amazing stretchy thing in bed first thing in the morning. Let your partner stimulate you, and surrender to it. Cook a lovely meal for yourself. Experience all the pleasure you're so worthy of.

rediscovering pleasure

A list of 10 little things that bring me pleasure:

1. ....

2. ....

3. ....

4. ....

5. ....

6. ....

7. ....

8. ....

9. ....

10. ....

Now make a list of all the things your body has gotten you through. If you've been in love, think about the butterflies in your tummy and the hot feeling you'd get when that person touched you. If you've had a child, think about the MIRACLE your body created in 9 months, growing a real human being from two tiny cells inside you! Think about all the mountains you've climbed, miles you've walked, orgasms you've had, tears you've cried, places you've explored, foods you've tasted, belly laughs you've had with your best friends, and healing you've done. None of this would be possible without the miracle of your body.

a list of pleasures my body lets me do, see, feel, and experience:

1. ....

2. ....

3. ....

4. ....

5. ....

6. ....

7. ....

8. ....

9. ....

10. ....

Everything good in this life you experience because of your body. So it's time to appreciate it, reconnect to it, and realize that although you are so much more than your body, you are also blessed to have one.

SELF-LOVE CHALLENGE
touch yourself

When was the last time you touched yourself just to feel yourself (not necessarily in the sexual sense, although that's always an option!)? You may be so caught up with looking at your body that you forget to feel in your body. So try it: Wrap your arms around your body and give yourself a loving hug. Put your hands on your stomach and picture the trillions of cells working to keep you alive. Grab your thighs and feel their strength. Touch every part of your body you've ever criticized, and let the touch of your hands reconnect you to all your body does for you. As you do this, close your eyes and send love to each area. Keep sending love until acceptance comes.

Write about this experience below.

when I touched my body, I felt ...

↓

_____
_____
_____
_____
_____
_____
_____
_____
_____
_____

eating intuitively

Every day, you have the opportunity to experience one of life's simplest pleasures: eating a meal. Whether it's your go-to coffee and bagel for breakfast, a quick lunch out with your colleagues, or a delicious dinner with your family, eating is not only something you must do to stay alive, but also something you should enjoy while you're doing it.

As a baby, you are born eager to eat, and as a child, food is usually a source of fun! From cake at birthdays to peanut butter sandwiches in your lunch box, you looked forward to snacks and mealtimes, because food made you happy. As a kid, you probably ate much differently than you do now. And I'm not talking about what you ate; I'm talking about how you ate.

Think back to how you used to eat as a small child. You probably ate what your parents or caretakers gave you, sometimes finishing your meal, sometimes not. At times, you'd forget about food altogether, because you were too preoccupied with playing on the playground or focused on completing your arts and crafts. Other times, you'd look forward to dinner, because you knew your mom was making your favorite—spaghetti. It was so tasty that you'd ask for seconds and then find yourself feeling a bit stuffed, but it was OK, because the meal was so yummy.

Overall, you practiced intuitive eating without even realizing it. Even though your eating wasn't "perfect," you didn't beat yourself up for eating a little too much, nor did you label your food as "good" or "bad." If anything, ice cream was "good" because it made you happy, and spinach was "bad" because it wasn't as tasty! You weren't preoccupied with thoughts about food, but you looked forward to a delicious meal. You ate when you felt hungry and stopped when you felt full. You were in harmony with your body's needs and wants.

As you grew older, you stopped trusting your body to tell you when, what, and how much to eat and resorted to following the messages of the diet-obsessed world: Eat this and not that, count your calories and track your macros, eat to shrink your body instead of eating for nourishment. These toxic messages about food, weight, and your body take away from what eating is supposed to be: a soulful, enjoyable experience that connects you to your body.

The good news is, you can always go back to eating like you did when you were a child. Intuitive eating, formally introduced by Evelyn Tribole and Elyse Resch in their book by the same name, is a non-diet way of eating that embraces listening to your body. This approach makes YOU the expert of your body's signals. Instead of following arbitrary food rules, diets, or meal plans, which often lead to restriction, deprivation, and dissatisfaction, you'll start reconnecting to your body's innate wisdom. Even though this may feel like a novel approach to food, it's going back to the basics.

Now I know what you're thinking: *Mary, if I eat whatever I want, then I'll just be eating pizza and ice cream all day! That can't be healthy!*

The short answer: No, you won't. It seems that way now, because you probably have strong cravings for "forbidden foods," but this is only because they're forbidden. It's like telling a toddler, "No, you can't have that." What do they do? They throw a tantrum, because telling a kid they can't have something makes them want it more! Adults are the same way.

At first, when you're not used to intuitive eating, you may find yourself gravitating toward more of those foods you used to restrict. When I was (re)learning to eat intuitively, I remember going through a period when I craved spoonfuls of peanut butter and could easily kill a whole jar in one sitting. But it was only because I "couldn't" (read: wouldn't) have it during my days of extreme dieting. This phase passed, because I stopped forbidding myself my favorite foods, and now, I feel totally neutral about peanut butter! I can have a jar in my pantry for months without even wanting it.

When you consistently listen to your body and give it time to start trusting you to honor its needs and wants, you'll find that your body will crave balance. It will ask you for nutrient-dense foods because they make you feel good and it will ask you to honor cravings because they will make you happy.

I want to emphasize that unlearning years, if not decades, of diet mentality will take time. You might have slip-ups where you eat too much and feel guilty about it. Or you might find yourself still feeling hungry and wishing you had some more of this or that. This is normal! Remind yourself that every feeling of discomfort is just your body gently reminding you what it needs more of less of. Intuitive eating is not about eating perfectly, but rather reconnecting to your body, finding balance and harmony, and getting pleasure from food again.

 how to eat intuitively

Envision a full day of intuitive eating. What would you eat? More importantly, how would you feel while you ate?

Think about savoring a bite of your favorite food. How does it taste? Smell? What's the texture? How do you feel when you eat it? Does it invite pleasure? That is how intuitive eating feels.

Now that you can imagine what intuitive eating looks and feels like for you personally, here are some tips for putting it into practice. (Note: These principles are inspired by the official *Intuitive Eating* book and program, available online.)

1. Let go of dieting. Intuitive eating is the opposite of dieting; they cannot coexist. If you want to give intuitive eating a chance, you must commit to not dieting. I know it can be tempting to start another diet, especially on those negative-body-image days, but DON'T DO IT. You've probably been dieting—or thinking about dieting—for a long time, so try something different for once. Are you ready to let go of dieting and start having the joy, freedom, and peace with food that comes from intuitive eating?

2. Try not to use words like "good" or "bad" to describe your eating, and don't say things like, "Ugh, I'm so bad for eating this cake!" or, "I'm being good today because I'm eating a salad!" Giving food moral value brings on feelings of guilt and shame, which are the opposite of the feelings you're aiming for: pleasure and enjoyment. Cake is "good" if you're enjoying it without guilt, and salad can be "bad" if you're ignoring your body's needs and only eating it because you feel you "should."

**health is not just about what you're putting in your body;
it's also about what you're thinking and saying to yourself.**

3. Honor your health. You know what's healthy for your body, so trust yourself to make food choices that nourish your body and make you feel good. Remember that one snack or meal is not going to make or break your health, so you don't have to eat perfectly to be healthy.

4. Pay attention to your hunger and fullness cues. Keep your body fed, and don't let yourself get too hungry. Excessive hunger usually leads to eating quickly and mindlessly, driving you to overeat. When you eat, check in with your body to make sure you stop before your fullness becomes uncomfortable. If you unintentionally forget to eat or accidentally overeat, ditch the guilt and remind yourself that it's about progress, not perfection.

5. Practice patience, kindness, and trust for your body. The best part about intuitive eating is that it's a constant practice of self-compassion. It's about learning to treat your body nicely and giving it what it's asking for. This process takes time, but it's worth it for the feelings of peace, pleasure, and freedom you'll start to feel around food.

Emotional eating is something that gets a bad rap in diet culture. It seems to equate to weakness or a lack of discipline.

Intuitive eating, on the other hand, does not shame emotional eating, because it recognizes that eating is inherently emotional! You have cake at birthday parties to celebrate a person's life. You go to happy hours with your colleagues to release stress from work and feel more cheerful for the weekend. You have a smoothie for breakfast to feel more energized for the day. You go out on dinner dates to connect and enjoy each other's company. You cuddle up on the couch with a bowl of popcorn and a movie to feel cozy and relaxed. All of these scenarios revolve around food and also involve your moods, feelings, and emotions.

Hopefully, most of the emotions you experience around food are positive; that's a big part of intuitive eating. But you're not a weak or horrible person for turning to food when you're down too. You can't deny that sometimes, warm cookies do make you feel better when you're sad and munching on chips is satisfying when you're stressed. I'm not condoning trying to drown your sorrows in a pint of ice cream every night, but instead pointing out that emotional eating is not as bad as it's made out to be. As long as it's not the only way you cope with your feelings, food can provide you with the quick comfort you need to feel better. So go easy on yourself.

Instead of trying to resist emotional eating, recognize that nearly all eating is emotional. The key is to try to minimize the negative emotions around food—guilt, shame, anxiety—and channel more positive emotions around food—pleasure, comfort, enjoyment.

dealing with weight gain (or the fear of it)

If you've been on a restrictive diet before, one by-product of intuitive eating may be some weight gain. It's normal for your weight to go up after you quit dieting. Since you've been depriving your body for so long, it's only natural for it to hold on to the calories and nutrients you're finally giving it (weight gain is actually one of the long-term effects of dieting, but nobody tells you that when they're selling you the diet). And I'm here to tell you that this is NOT A BAD THING. I know it sounds scary—trust me, I've been there. I'm not exaggerating when I tell you that my biggest fear used to be gaining weight. (No, really, if you would've asked me 3 years ago what I was most scared of, I wouldn't say sharks or losing a family member; I'd say, "Getting fat.")

It's not my fault this was my biggest fear. And if it's one of your fears, it's not your fault either. This is a direct reflection of how people have been programmed by society. But like I always say, the pain was not your fault, but the healing is your responsibility. It's your responsibility because gaining weight, in and of itself, is not a bad thing and is often an important part of your self-love journey.

Let's examine some common fears about weight gain—and how they are actually false.

fear #1: gaining weight is unhealthy, and losing weight will make you healthier.

I was challenged by this idea for quite some time, especially after I quit bikini competitions. As I watched my body gain more weight in one summer than I did during all of puberty, I felt so heavy, lethargic, and depressed that I thought, *There's NO WAY that this is healthy for me.*

But did I feel unhealthy because of the extra weight OR because I let myself feel so stressed, anxious, and ashamed about the weight gain?

Maybe gaining weight is your body's natural process of coming to a healthy weight range. I don't know your weight or health status, but what I do know, based on scientific research, is that restrictive dieting is not healthy. Experts in "obesity" have concluded that dieters who manage to sustain their weight loss are the exception, not the rule, and dieters who gain back more weight than they lost may very well be the norm.

side note: I use the term "obesity" because it is widely recognized, although I do not necessarily agree with this kind of weight classification because it comes with a lot of damaging stigma.

Not only do most dieters gain back more weight than they lost, but there is evidence that this kind of weight cycling leads to increased cardiovascular disease, heart attack, stroke, and diabetes and even suppressed immune function. Not to mention trying to achieve the "perfect" body often leads to myriad of mental health battles including poor body image (which can lead to eating disorders), preoccupation with food (which can lead to anxiety), and low self-esteem (which can lead to depression).

To take this further, "thin" does not equate to "healthy," and "fat" does not equate to "unhealthy." Think of a marketing image of a thin person eating a burger. Chances are, people don't assume this person is unhealthy, even though this thin person could eat red meat every day, smoke, and drink alcohol and soda all the time! The physical body alone can't reveal someone's health, but you've been brainwashed to think that it can.

Now picture the same image but with a person with a larger body eating a burger. Chances are, you'd see comments like, "She's promoting obesity" or "She needs to stop eating burgers and go on a diet." Meanwhile, this person could be infinitely healthier in body, mind, and spirit than the thin person.

There is so much more going on inside someone than can be seen on the outside. When I was at my lowest weight, for example, I had vitamin and nutrient deficiencies in nearly every category and multiple kidney infections from all the protein powders I was drinking, and I would nearly fall asleep while driving because I was so exhausted! Now, at a higher weight, I'm healthier than I've ever been in my life. All my blood work shows it, and I feel good physically and mentally.

Not everyone who loses weight or lives in a smaller body is healthy, and not everyone who gains weight or lives in a bigger body is unhealthy. We cannot make those kinds of blanket statements about health and weight. There is so much to health that we can't see that we need to stop making snap judgments and consider the whole picture, including spiritual, emotional, and mental health. (More on this later!)

On that note, we all know that stress is the No. 1 killer, and stressing out about your body is, well, stressful! Studies show that the shame and stress we feel while trying so hard to lose weight can be much worse for us than actually carrying extra weight.

It's our job to stop these misconceptions about thin/fat and healthy/unhealthy. We need to encourage a more nuanced and holistic approach to body size and health. Here are some key points to remember:

✦ we cannot make assumptions about someone's health based on their body size, shape, or weight.
✦ thin does not equal healthy, and fat does not equal unhealthy. so gaining weight will not automatically make you unhealthy.
✦ health is about much, much more than weight.

fear #2: if i gain weight, then i won't be attractive (and no one will like me and i'll die alone).

A big part of why I was obsessed with making my body thinner and fitter is because I was chasing external validation. I wanted more people to like me, be interested in me, and find me attractive (especially men). I got high off compliments about my body, because it made me feel like I was doing something right. But of course, this high was short-lived and followed by the pressure to maintain that look or find something else to "improve" about my appearance, which ultimately left me feeling empty inside.

When I cared a lot about how I looked and lived my life wanting other people to like how I looked, I naturally attracted men who cared about how I looked. Sure, these men would appreciate my body at first, but they were the same men who criticized my body, gave me backhanded compliments, and made me feel like they only liked me for how I looked. I remember one time a guy told me that I was "cute, but a little too fluffy for his liking." After I gained some weight, another guy told me, "I'm so glad you're not skinny anymore. I don't like skinny girls," which was especially hurtful because we dated when I was "skinny" too. It felt like my body was never good enough for these shallow, narrow-minded people.

I wish someone had told me back then:

your attractiveness is not dependent on your weight, and anyone who thinks so doesn't deserve you.

Remember: There is someone out there for everyone, and every BODY—both sexually and romantically. People who are worthy of loving you will love you no matter how much you weigh. You are beautiful and attractive as you are. Period. End of story.

fear #3: gaining weight means you've "given up on yourself," "let yourself go," or "gotten lazy."

When I first quit dieting, these thoughts ran rampant in my mind. Not a single moment passed when I didn't feel guilty for something I ate or skipping a workout or "losing control" around food. I was one of many people who equated being thin with self-control, motivation, and productivity.

So naturally, I thought gaining weight would mean I was the opposite: out of control, lazy, and unproductive.

Refusing to succumb to society's unrealistic beauty expectations is not giving up on yourself. It takes a tremendous amount of strength and integrity. And finding other—better—things to do with your time, energy, and money besides pursuing weight loss is not lazy. It's infinitely more productive, for both you and the collective you.

One thing that can help you do this is to think about some of the people you look up to who don't fit into society's cookie-cutter beauty standard. (Mine include Mother Teresa, Maya Angelou, Anne Frank, Rosa Parks, Michelle Obama, Chimamanda Ngozi Adichie, Lady Gaga, Malala Yousafzai, and many, many more.)

list five names that come to mind. reflect on all these people have accomplished, and write down what you admire about them.

1. _____
_____
_____
_____
_____

2. _____
_____
_____
_____
_____

3. _____
_____
_____
_____
_____

4. _____
_____
_____
_____
_____

5. _____
_____
_____
_____
_____

Now ask yourself, do any of their accomplishments have anything to do with their weight? Are their looks what people remember them for and look up to them for? Would you call them lazy just because they don't look like your typical fitness model on Instagram?

hell no.

Gaining weight was the starting point for doing bigger and better things with my life. Instead of spending 4 hours at the gym, I started to take my schoolwork more seriously, reading, writing, and studying for my degree. Instead of spending money on diet supplements, I spent it traveling the world and sharing experiences and adventures with my friends. I finally had the energy and brain space to do things I wanted to do, because my mind was not consumed by what I was going to eat next or if I looked "fat" in a certain outfit.

Sure, my body looked different, because my priorities were different: I valued precious moments with my friends, family, and myself more than I valued the number on the scale.

In short, when I gained weight, I gained LIFE. And I would do it all over again.

Self-love opens up time for the things that will stimulate you mentally and spiritually. So, is there a new hobby you want to take on? Books you've always wanted to read? A subject you've always wanted to study? Spend more time doing those things, because you want your precious energy to flow into healing, positive, and empowering activities. Where attention goes, energy flows.

stop "feeling fat" and start feeling your feelings

If I put on jeans and they were too tight, I used to instantly think, *I feel fat*. And that thought would send me in a downward spiral of self-hate, because at the time, I thought "fat" was the worst thing someone could be. (No one had taught me that fat was OK, that fat wasn't bad, and that fat had nothing to do with lack of health, worth, or love.) "I feel fat" was the go-to feeling, but "fat" wasn't the root issue here.

Every time we think something negative about our body or appearance, it's usually about something else having to do with self-worth or a deep wound or insecurity from the past.

When someone or something triggers us into thinking we're not good enough, we can instantly connect that to feeling fat, so we think the solution is to get thinner, without examining our underlying feelings.

So we start a diet or "detox" or eat clean or drink coffee with the hopes of suppressing appetite or take a laxative or do extra cardio or starve or suck in our tummies or put on Spanx or YOU NAME IT.

We succumb to all the harmful methods we use to stop "feeling fat."

Maybe they work short term and you get a small boost in confidence, but over the long term these things don't work! Why?

Well, because all these methods address only the external problem. But "feeling fat" is not an external problem with your body.

It's also not even a feeling! "Fat" is a word we use to describe our negative self-worth, because it's so much easier to say "I feel fat" than it is to say, "I am struggling with my body image, because I'm scared that if I don't live up to other people's expectations, they'll judge me and not find me attractive and not want to hang out with me, so I'm actually scared of rejection and loneliness."

Aah, now that's some deep shit right there.

When we don't know how to express and process our emotions, and love ourselves through the process, we resort to blaming our beautiful bodies. So please, for the love of whoever or whatever you believe in, stop saying, "I feel fat."

Not only is this statement preventing you from identifying and processing your true feelings, but it also contributes to society's toxic view of bodies. Here are three good reasons to stop

1. It makes fat seem like the worst thing you can possibly be (which you now know it's not).

2. It disregards your true, underlying feelings of low self-worth, and it convinces you that fixing your body will help. (If you've ever lost weight and still felt you needed to lose more, that's a prime example.)

3. It's insulting to people who may have bigger bodies than you. If you feel fat, how are other people who are even slightly bigger than you supposed to feel? It's inconsiderate to go around saying this.

The next few pages will help you process your true feelings and emotions. Next time you have a negative thought about your body or appearance, pull out this exercise.

fat is not a feeling

Right now, I feel ...
(Circle one or add your own.)

unworthy	anxious	beaten down
sad	afraid	moody
depressed	nervous	lost
lethargic	rejected	lonely
exhausted	unloved	misunderstood
tired	stressed	resentful
_____	_____	_____

now brain-dump anything and everything else you're feeling. let it all out.

_____

_____

_____

_____

_____

_____

_____

_____

i have these negative feelings because ...

_____
_____
_____
_____
_____
_____
_____
_____
_____

sometimes, i blame my body for my negative feelings because ...

_____
_____
_____
_____
_____
_____
_____
_____
_____
_____

i know my body is NOT the cause of these negative feelings because ...

(think about the times you've successfully changed your body and still felt negative feelings, or reflect on how your self-worth struggles are so much deeper than your appearance.)

_____
_____
_____
_____
_____
_____

right now, i am most afraid that ...

_____
_____
_____
_____
_____
_____

a better way to process my feelings would be ...

_____
_____
_____
_____
_____
_____

Phew! I hope you felt that catharsis that comes with processing your true feelings and emotions, rather than putting a bandage on them and disguising them as "feeling fat."

Remember: Saying, "I feel fat" is just another way to avoid confronting your true thoughts, feelings, and emotions. Once you get real with how you feel, you'll be able to heal.

health at every size

Eating disorders have the highest mortality rate of any mental illness. And weight loss is a symptom of many mental and physical health conditions, including depression, diabetes, thyroid problems, HIV/AIDS, and cancer. But for some odd reason, society continues to idolize weight loss as if it's the best thing a person can achieve.

The way society treats people in larger bodies is something the Health at Every Size movement (HAES) aims to tackle. The HAES principles were created by the Association for Size Diversity and Health (ASDAH) and promote the idea that health should be treated holistically and independent of one's body size. They push for weight inclusivity by not idealizing or pathologizing specific weights or body sizes. HAES advocates for equal access to health care and respect toward everyone, no matter their body size, shape, weight, or ability.

It's important to note that HAES does not imply healthy at every size. HAES does not claim everyone is healthy but rather that everyone should have access to health-care without stigma.

This means that someone in a bigger body should be able to go to the doctor and get fair, equal, and appropriate treatment for their symptoms without anyone telling them to "just lose weight" or face the judgment and discrimination that fat people hear on a daily basis.

I discovered HAES during my eating disorder recovery journey. I was desperate for some sort of medical advice that would tell me something other than to go on another diet and try to lose weight. I wanted something that took mental health, emotional well-being, and other people's bodies into consideration rather than focusing solely on the physical. HAES was a godsend to me. It expanded my definition of health and gave me permission to accept my body at any size, shape, weight, or ability.

HAES grounds itself in a social justice framework that takes into account complex social and cultural identities, issues of accessibility, and individual needs and desires—all of which must be taken into consideration when thinking about our health.

HAES is a great resource if you're on a journey of balancing health and self-love.

true health

I used to think being healthy meant eating salads for every meal—hold the dressing!—and working out multiple hours per day. It never occurred to me that health was more than just physical.

Gaining weight was the healthiest thing for me. When I gained weight, I also gained happiness, insight, and experiences. I gained a more well-rounded, holistic approach to health. I embody health in a totally different way now, because my well-being includes my physical, mental, emotional, and spiritual health.

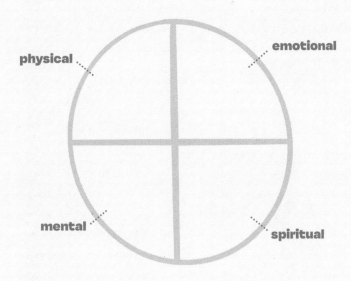

And when it comes to physical health, if dieting is not healthy, then how can you be healthy?

There are two crucial components to holistic physical health:

✦ your mindset about health
✦ your habits

That's right. Health is not the number on the scale or your jeans size; health is about what you're thinking, saying, and doing.

healthy mindset

Guess what? You already know exactly what healthy feels like to you. Even if you don't have a formal education in health, fitness, or nutrition, there is so much you do know when you connect to your body.

You know what foods do and do not make your body happy.

You know what types of movement make you feel energized and what types of workouts make you feel drained.

You know when you're thirsty, and you know when you need more rest.

You know a lot more about your body than society has made you believe. The answers do not lie in a magazine article, with a personal trainer, or in a fad diet. The answers lie within you.

Having a healthy mindset involves shifting your thinking about health and trusting your body. Say to yourself: I know what is best for my body, and I will do my best at trusting my body and taking care of it. I know that health is not just physical but also mental, emotional, and spiritual, and I will keep this in mind when making choices for myself and my body. I will practice intuitive eating and exercising in a way that truly makes me feel good. My health is not dependent on a number but rather on how I feel about myself and what I do to take care of my temple.

healthy habits

Just as that green smoothie will not automatically make you healthy, that extra slice of pizza also won't make you unhealthy. It's what you do over the long term that matters, which is why it's so important to create habits that you enjoy, because you're that much more likely to stick with them.

On the next page is a habit tracker of only some habits that will probably make you feel good. These are definitely not all of them, as health is super personal and individualized, but you can use this habit tracker as a starting point to help you reconnect to your body, listen to what it needs, and trust it a little more each day.

7-day tracker:

~~~~~~

- ☐ ate at least 2 servings of veggies

- ☐ drank at least 8 cups of water

- ☐ cooked a meal at home

- ☐ moved my body for at least 20 minutes

- ☐ did something kind for myself

- ☐ got 8 hours of good sleep

- ☐ spent time in meditation, prayer, or stillness

make your own:

~~~~~~

☐ _____

☐ _____

☐ _____

☐ _____

☐ _____

☐ _____

☐ _____

part three

bringing it all together

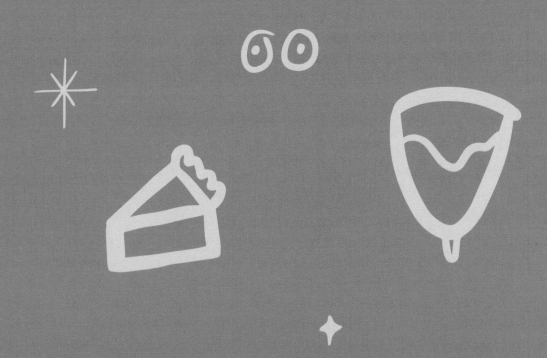

chapter 7
positive self-talk

positive self-talk

No matter how long you've been on your self-love journey, you will always experience twists and turns, hills and valleys, good times and not-so-good times. One day you might be wearing a bikini at the beach, feeling amazing, not caring what others think, and the next day you might feel like you got hit by a truck—a truck full of insecurities, self-doubt, and negative energy.

Everyone goes through this. Outside of the work you're doing in this book, real life is happening. And real life has contrast. Good and bad. Light and dark. Positive and negative. You must embrace this contrast and learn how to manage your mind in all situations. You need the right tools to approach those not-so-good days with self-compassion instead of self-criticism.

The most important tool for these moments is positive self-talk. I touched on this earlier in the book when I spoke about self-compassion and showing yourself kindness, but now I want to get into the details of how it works and how powerful it is. Even if you understand why you should love yourself, that doesn't mean that you'll magically start seeing yourself in a more positive light. It takes a little bit more work than that, and the work involves managing your mind.

You're dealing with your thoughts every day. You can't run away from them, no matter how much you try to distract yourself and stay busy. You can't pretend your thoughts don't affect you. They do. But how you manage them, what you say to yourself about them, and what you speak out loud to others can make all the difference.

···················· **don't believe everything you think** ····················

Ugh I had all these things on my to-do list, but it's 4 PM and I haven't gotten anything done! I suck at productivity.

I gained so much weight during my vacation! I can't believe I let myself go like this. Everyone is going to notice and think I fell off the wagon. I need to skip dinner tonight and start a diet tomorrow, so I don't get even fatter.

My partner is being kind of quiet tonight and seems upset. Did I do something wrong? What are they thinking? It's probably something bad about me.

Have you ever caught yourself thinking negative thoughts along those lines? You may be so used to this kind of internal negative chatter that you don't even notice it!

Why do you do this to yourself? Sadly, negative thoughts are ingrained in your DNA, because, since the beginning of humanity, the mind is prepared for the worst-case scenario to ensure survival. Your brain puts you on high alert for any potential danger, such as being attacked by a lion or tiger or bear, because if you're not prepared, then you'll get caught off guard when it jumps out to get you.

Now I don't know about you, but I have never found myself in a situation where I needed to run from a lion or tiger or bear. So most of my negative thoughts aren't in proportion to the things that are actually happening. If you keep track of all your negative thoughts for even just one day, you'll probably notice that most of them are not realistic or factual. A lot of them are just the result of your brain spiraling out of control and making up all these worst-case scenarios that will never happen. It isn't your brain's fault, but it is your responsibility to learn how to manage this cycle.

THOUGHTS → FEELINGS → EMOTIONS

According to psychologists, feelings are experienced consciously, meaning you usually know how you feel. Emotions, on the other hand, can be experienced either consciously or sub-consciously, and they're usually longer lasting. For example, hating your father is an emotion, because it's likely something that's been years in the making. Feeling frustrated with your dad because he won't go to the doctor is more of a feeling, because it's very much in the moment. Basically, emotions have much more energy behind them than day-to-day feelings, which are driven by thoughts.

For example, if you constantly think negatively about your body, then those thoughts will transform into negative feelings about your body. They will also trickle into other areas of your life, such as how comfortable you are voicing your opinion, how confident you feel taking on new projects or challenges, or how worthy you feel of love. Over time, these feelings will transform into emotions, which are more permanent and a lot harder to work through. The more negative emotions you feel over time, the more negative your thinking becomes, in an endless, vicious cycle.

So the diagram is actually more cyclical, like this:

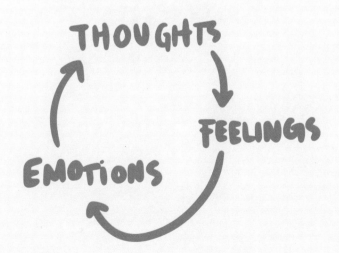

To end the vicious cycle, you must start by becoming aware of your thoughts and choosing to think differently. It's not about always thinking positively and never having a negative thought again, but rather about knowing you can choose which thoughts you listen to.

It's like my dog: Sometimes I call his name and he chooses not to pay attention. But if he hears the sound of his metal bowl banging against the countertop and the bag of kibble being opened, he comes bolting. Selective listening, right?

In the same way, you can use selective thinking. You hold the power to carefully filter your thoughts, not take all of them to heart, and create new, more empowering thoughts on a daily basis.

Take a few moments to think about your thinking. Sounds weird, right? Good. Do it anyway.

think about your thoughts:

What negative thoughts have come up for you in the past 24 hours? Write down the top five negative thoughts you've experienced in the past day or so.

1. _____
2. _____
3. _____
4. _____
5. _____

are any of these thoughts familiar—meaning, have you thought these thoughts before?

◯ *yes*　◯ *no*

do you feel like any of these negative thoughts have contributed to negative emotions? if so, which ones?

_____

_____

_____

_____

_____

_____

Before I talk about how to reframe your negative thoughts, I want you to know that what you are experiencing is normal. The specifics may differ, but there is not a single overriding thought you could be thinking that someone else hasn't thought before. So you are not alone in this, nor are you silly, stupid, or weird for anything you're thinking. The fact that you are becoming aware of your negative thoughts and not avoiding them is an act of courage.

neutral thinking

In 10th grade, I saw a picture on Pinterest of a girl looking at herself in the mirror. All over the mirror, she had Post-it notes that said things like, "You are beautiful" and "Yes, you can!" The idea was that if you looked at positive words each day, like she did, you'd naturally find yourself feeling more positive about yourself.

So, guess what I did later that day. I covered my mirror in Post-it notes with those same kinds of affirmations. I wrote, "I love my body" and "I am beautiful." (Back then, I still thought being physically attractive was the goal.)

A few days later, I found myself in front of the same mirror, looking at myself and hating everything I saw. Everything. I didn't hate only my tummy and thighs. I hated my whole personality for not making me the type of person who could be popular. I also blamed my family situation for not making me more "normal." Meanwhile, those sticky notes with the "positive" messages on my mirror? They made me feel worse! I didn't believe the words I wrote on them, so looking at them just made me feel like positive thinking was another thing I wasn't good at. So I gave up and went right back to feeling shitty.

Maybe you've had an experience like this, where you tried to think positively, but it didn't work. And that made you feel worse.

You'd think with all those cute motivational quotes all over social media these days, everyone would be feeling better about themselves. You know, the ones that say "Love Yourself!" or "Know Your Worth!" They're the digital equivalent of those Post-It notes. And while I think posting and practicing positive affirmations is helpful, sometimes it feels like those messages will never be enough to silence the voice inside our heads. The voice that won't stop telling us to hate ourselves.

It can be incredibly invalidating when someone does not acknowledge where you're at and makes it seem like #goodvibesonly is the solution. You know, "Just think positive!" It's frustrating. And it can even make you feel more negative. I find that empty affirmations—whether on Post-it notes or against a pretty Instagram filter—are similar, almost like they're encouraging you to ignore your true feelings and replace them with sunny, often hard-to-believe affirmations instead.

If affirmations work for you, great! But if they don't, you might want to try a different approach—one that has worked much better for me and for hundreds of women I've coached. Instead of putting pressure on yourself to replace negative thoughts with positive ones, try to replace negative thoughts with neutral thoughts. In doing this, you meet your brain halfway. It's like saying, "Look, your negativity is totally unrealistic, and here's why" instead of "Your negativity is totally unrealistic, so I'm going to slap a positivity Band-Aid on top of it and hope for the best."

Replacing a negative thought with a neutral thought feels a lot more real and true and possible.

For example, if you're having bad body-image thoughts, instead of forcing yourself to repeat, *I love my body*, tell yourself, *I am learning to love my body*.

If you're feeling overwhelmed with school and work and family and life, don't try to pretend everything is all good and Zen. Instead, acknowledge what you're feeling, practice self-compassion, and say to yourself, I am juggling a lot right now, so of course I'm going to be stressed. I'm going to ask someone for help or to take something off my plate.

negative thought vs. neutral thought

negative thought	neutral thought
✦ I hate my body.	✦ I am learning to love my body.
✦ I can't handle this.	✦ I have handled difficult things before, and I can handle this too.
✦ I will always feel insecure.	✦ As long as I keep working on my confidence, I will keep making improvements.
✦ I can't believe I failed that exam! I'm so stupid!	✦ Failure is a part of learning. One failed exam is not the end of the world, and I will have many more chances to succeed in the future.

You can see that the neutral thought is not positive or negative. And it's also more realistic. You're not trying to trick yourself into thinking that you love your body when you don't, or that you feel totally confident when in reality you want to crawl in a hole and hide. Instead, you're meeting your thoughts halfway and giving yourself the time, space, and grace to be a work in progress.

Because we are ALWAYS a work in progress.

neutralize the negative

On the left-hand side of the space below, brain-dump a few negative thoughts that have come up for you in the past week or so. No matter how silly or stupid it feels, write down every single negative thought that comes to mind. Start with the ones you jotted down earlier, and then add any others that you want to release from your subconscious. Think of this as a cleanse. Releasing the negative thoughts onto paper makes them a lot more manageable, because now you can face them. It's important that you fill up the left column completely before moving on to the right.

After you've dumped your negative thoughts into the left column, go to the right column and neutralize those thoughts. This may take some time, especially if the negative thought feels very real to you. You may have been talking shit to yourself for so long that it's hard to stop. It's OK. Sit with it for a while, or skip that thought and get back to it at the end. Use phrases like, "I'm learning to ..." or "I'm working on ..." or "I'm practicing ..." to begin your neutral thoughts.

negative thought   ## *neutral thought*

_____   _____

_____   _____

_____   _____

_____   _____

_____   _____

_____   _____

the gift of self-love

_____   _____
_____   _____
_____   _____
_____   _____
_____   _____
_____   _____
_____   _____
_____   _____
_____   _____
_____   _____
_____   _____
_____   _____
_____   _____
_____   _____
_____   _____
_____   _____
_____   _____
_____   _____
_____   _____

YOU GOT THIS!

thinking out loud

Have you ever heard or participated in a conversation that goes something like this?

"Ugh! I wish my legs were toned like yours!"

"OMG, are you kidding? Have you seen mine? They're terrible! Look how flabby!"

"No way, yours are perfect! But mine are so big, and I hate them."

Maybe you've had this kind of conversation with a friend. Or maybe you've heard another group of girls having it, going on and on in this competition of self-deprecation and trying to make each other feel better. But this does a lot more harm than good.

I used to talk with my girlfriends like this all the time. It didn't matter if we were discussing our body "imperfections," comparing how well we did on an exam ("I did so bad!" / "No way, you're so much smarter than me, but I definitely failed."), or talking about our personalities ("You're so cool and outgoing when we go out, and I'm like an awkward gremlin!").

It may seem harmless, but we do it so much that we don't even recognize the damage we're doing. I mean, what can be so bad about telling your best friend that you don't want to leave the house today because your hair looks bad? Aren't you just telling the truth?

Well, remember how I talked about society's beauty standards in chapters 5 and 6? When you verbalize your negative beliefs about your looks to your friends, you reinforce the idea that your looks matter, that if you don't look up to par, then you shouldn't go on to live your life. It feels extreme, I know. But these small conversations add up and play a big part in perpetuating society's harmful expectations of women. To be honest, I've never heard a group of guys talking about their insecurities or flaws as nonchalantly as women do. And why do you think that is?

Women are trained to talk negatively both to themselves and about themselves. Conversations with others simply show how socially acceptable it is for women to be mean to themselves—as long as they're nice to others, of course. Negative self-talk has become such second nature that women don't even blink an eye when someone else does it out loud.

When you verbalize these negative thoughts, you're giving them more power and doing harm to yourself AND those around you. When you say something negative about yourself, your best friend may then start questioning whether she looks good enough to go out. Even if she feels like she does, you still reminded her that her looks matter, so now she'll likely be thinking about that throughout the night.

So first and foremost, try to be conscientious about the words you choose to talk about yourself, especially around your friends. This can be done simply by setting an intention for your interactions like: "My intention is to inspire the people around me to be kinder to themselves by only speaking kind words about myself."

Then, if you hear others putting themselves down, practice responding in a way that validates their feelings but doesn't contribute to the negative things they say about themselves. Saying, "Oh, stop! You're beautiful!" is invalidating to the other person's feelings, no matter how much you mean it. Instead, it's better to acknowledge what they're feeling and do a simple rephrase: "I know you don't feel beautiful right now, but I always think you're beautiful both inside and out." How much more empowering does that sound?

I know you want to make your friends feel better about their "flaws," and sometimes it feels like the easiest way to do that is to show them that you also feel insecure about your "flaws." Of course, it's helpful to feel like you're not alone in your insecurities, but this only gives a temporary sense of peace. So if your friend is putting herself down and you feel you need to contribute by verbalizing your own negative thoughts, try instead to say something like, "I also have a hard time accepting my body as it is, but I'm learning to practice better self-talk." Notice how you're using the same neutral language I talked about earlier (e.g., "I'm learning to ...")." Now you're extending the gift of self-love to other people with a simple shift in your language. Just as you're shifting the thoughts in your head.

To truly empower someone else, you must empower yourself. Don't participate in conversations that make you compare yourself with others, self-deprecate in an attempt to make someone feel better, or fuel what you don't like about yourself. Instead, respond with a neutral statement and invite your friends to practice kinder self-talk too.

SELF-LOVE CHALLENGE

watch what you say

How you talk to others is usually how you talk to yourself. For the next day, try not to not say anything critical about yourself out loud. If you need to express yourself, use the Neutralize the Negative exercise in the previous section to come up with statements that are less self-deprecating and more realistic to describe what you're dealing with.

your self-talk guide

Most of the messages I receive on Instagram or by email go something like this: *What can I tell myself to get over my ex? ... Do you have any advice for dealing with hating my body after gaining weight? ... I'm feeling really sad/lonely/stressed/depressed/etc. What can I do to stop feeling this way?*

What most people don't realize is that when you ask someone else for advice, words of encouragement, or tips, you're really looking for someone to teach you how to think. Even though the situations are different, everyone wants the same thing: to silence the negative voice inside and be more empowered.

When I respond to these emails, it's not like I have a secret self-love weapon that I've been hoarding for years, waiting for the right person to ask me so I can finally reveal it. I simply respond with my words, with the hope that when someone reads them, they'll hear my voice inside their head, reminding them they are enough, that whatever they're feeling is temporary, and that there are better days ahead. When I'm writing to them, all I can do is hope that my voice is louder than their inner critic, if only for a moment. That moment of positive self-talk could be the turning point for them.

It's the same with this book. I'm not telling you a secret. I'm not forcing you into loving yourself. I'm not even telling you anything revolutionary. What I'm doing is trying to help you think, see, and feel differently about yourself by shining light on a new perspective; giving you relevant information; and most important, empowering you to treat yourself as you would someone you love.

I know that sometimes it's nice to hear it from someone else, but all the answers are within you. You don't need anyone else to tell you you're good enough; you need to be able to say it to yourself. Even when it's hard. Even when you don't believe it. Even when it feels easier to listen to the nasty inner critic.

But like anything, positive self-talk takes practice. Maybe the first time you say something kind to yourself, you won't believe it right away. But the more you are kind to yourself, the more you'll believe in yourself and the more you'll be kind to yourself some more.

To really bring this concept of positive self-talk home, I want to give you a guide, like a little handbook, of what to say to yourself, depending on what negative thoughts you're having. This is literally what I would write to you if you sent me an email! Anything that I would say to you, you can say to yourself too. I mean, that's what self-talk is!

I invite you to put a bookmark or sticky note on this page so you can refer back to it anytime you're feeling down.

if you're feeling sad ...

This too shall pass. Nothing is permanent, including this feeling. You've been through diffi-culties before, and you've survived all of them. You probably even thrived, because those experiences helped shape you into a strong, resilient, and powerful person. Sadness helps happiness feel that much better. In fact, there would be no happiness if there weren't sad-ness. So, let this feeling be a signal that there are better days ahead.

if you're feeling stressed ...

I know that stress feels like a bad thing, but that's not always the case. Being stressed about something means you care about doing your best. Make sure you are rested. Rest is a priority, because it allows you to handle stressful situations in a calm manner. Take it one step at a time, because the only thing that matters is what you're doing right here, right now. Ask yourself what you can take off your plate or ask someone to help with. You are capable of handling whatever is on your mind or your to-do list, but it is always OK to ask for and receive help.

if you're feeling angry ...

Anger is a healthy feeling and emotion. It's important to process the anger so that it can move through you instead of being bottled up inside in a way that hurts you or comes out to hurt someone else. My favorite quote is, "It's OK to lose your shit sometimes, because if you keep your shit inside, you'll end up being full of shit. Then you'll explode, and there will be shit everywhere. It'll be a shitstorm, and nobody wants that." So don't be afraid to sometimes lose your shit. Write in your journal. Tear through the pages with your pen. Burn them when you're done. Ugly cry—like one of those screaming cries where the walls start to shake. If you're angry at someone, process your feelings first, and then let that person know how you truly feel. Let it out. Breathe. And most important, forgive yourself.

if you're feeling anxious before a test, performance, or big event ...

Did you know that anxiety and excitement feel the same in the body? Think about the last time you gave a big presentation and the first time you held your crush's hand. What did those two events have in common? Heart beating, stomach in knots, sweaty palms, right? A 2014 study from Harvard found that when you're anxious, instead of trying to tell yourself to calm down, it's a lot more effective to say to yourself, I am excited! to help your brain and body see that there's no physical threat, but rather a new opportunity.

if you're feeling anxious about the future ...

I know you know this, but the future doesn't exist. All we have is now. And right now, you're OK. Exactly where you are and exactly as you are. When anxiety comes up, it's important to thank it. It is actually trying to help you, because anxiety is how you deal with the threat of uncertainty. Tell your anxiety, "Thank you for trying to keep me safe, but I am OK right now." Anxiety can also distort your reality, making you catastrophize (Everything is going bad!), futurize (Everything will go bad!), or overgeneralize (Everything always goes bad!). These thoughts are not reality, but it will take some time to retrain your brain to recognize that.

Although sometimes, anxiety is there to tell us that something isn't right. Explore what that could be by taking some deep breaths, writing in your journal, and listening to your heart. It may seem hard right now, but it'll become easier and easier each time you practice turning an anxious thought into a neutral thought. You've got this.

if you're feeling lonely ...

Sometimes you can feel lonely in a room full of people, while other times you may feel totally content sitting alone in your room. What does that tell you? Loneliness is not situational but a feeling that comes from within. It's OK to feel lonely. Everyone feels lonely sometimes. When you're lonely, you have extra time to get to know your true self, outside of other people's agendas, opinions, and expectations. Loneliness doesn't mean others don't love you. It means you get to practice loving yourself a little more.

if you're feeling like you want to self-sabotage ...

We tend to sabotage when we don't feel worthy of good things—healthy love, success, abundance, recognition, healing, joy. But listen, you are worthy of all those things and more. Instead of beating yourself up for procrastinating or being tempted to fall into old habits, recognize that you are still learning to see your worth, and it's times like these that allow you to prove to yourself how strong you really are. Instead of beating yourself up, take note of your feelings and say, "Hmmm, that's interesting. My brain is feeling uncomfortable, so it wants to resort to old habits. Thanks, brain! I'm going to do my own thing now."

if you're feeling like you want to text your ex ...

Don't. It's normal to want to go back to the old, familiar, and comfortable when you're feeling down, but that doesn't mean you should act on that urge. There's a reason it didn't work out. This person came into your life to teach you something, but now it's time to take what you learned and move on. You deserve better. You deserve affection and romance and hot sex and unconditional love. You deserve someone who makes you feel seen, heard, and appreciated. You deserve the love you freely give to others.

Your thoughts can be just thoughts if you stop giving so much significance to them. You can choose the thoughts you listen to, so choose carefully. And your feelings can be felt and processed without becoming self-destructive. If a negative thought, feeling, or emotion comes up for you, acknowledge it, neutralize it, and then move on with your life. There is always a positive way to talk to yourself about your feelings, and it's usually the same way you would talk to a friend going through the same thing. What would you say to them? What is the truth beneath all the noise? Don't contribute to negative self-talk, whether it's happening in your head or in a conversation with a friend. Nip it in the bud quickly, change the topic, and whatever you do, don't text your ex.

chapter 8
radiating love

radiating love

Now that you've done so much valuable inner work, let's talk about how to own who you are and show up in the world as the most confident, empowered, badass version of yourself. At the beginning of this book, I talked about how self-love is not selfish, because it frees your brain space for other, more important things like connecting with others, focusing on your passions, and living your best life. By taking self-love outside yourself, you inspire those around you too. This creates a positive feedback loop that looks like this:

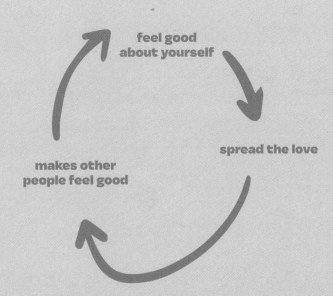

feel good
about yourself

spread the love

makes other
people feel good

Your love for yourself will deepen when you commit to doing little acts of self-love: accepting compliments, communicating your feelings, and staying true to who you are. All of these have the added bonus of empowering those around you to do the same.

···················· **stop apologizing** ····················

One day I was using the changing room at my yoga studio when a woman walked by my locker and said, "Oops! I'm sorry!"

The funny thing is, I didn't even notice her next to me until she apologized. She didn't even bump into me! She apologized simply because she was taking up space. And I'm sure she's not the only one who's done this.

Be honest with yourself here. Have you ever ...

✦ Sent a long email or text (over) explaining to your friend why you had to cancel plans and how you're so sorry but you'll make it up to her next time?

✦ Used an exclamation point or smiley face emoji at the end of a sentence so as not to come across as too assertive?

✦ Apologized to someone when you didn't even run into them, for simply "being in their way"?

If you don't think you're worthy of taking up space, making requests, and being bold, you end up spending your life tiptoeing around people, choosing your words too carefully, and apologizing for existing.

I've never seen men apologize for their existence like women do. It seems like men say what needs to be said and don't feel the need to overexplain themselves or apologize a million times. In fact, in a 2010 study done by *Psychological Science*, men and women kept a diary of all their "offenses" and whether or not they offered an apology. The women and men apologized the same amount, but the women reported more "offenses" for which they apologized. So it's not that men don't apologize; it's that their threshold of what's considered an "offense" or wrongdoing is much higher than women's. It seems that men don't feel the need to apologize for little things like not responding to a text right away or canceling plans, because they don't think they did anything wrong.

And I'm not saying you need to talk or act like men, because it's such a gift to be sensitive to other people's feelings. But perhaps there's something you can learn from this study. (News flash! Not responding to a text right away is not wrong!)

No more apologizing for the little things! The first step is to stop apologizing and start receiving.

Try this: Instead of saying, "I'm sorry," say, "Thank you"—e.g., "Thank you for understanding," "Thank you for being patient," "Thank you for taking the time," "Thank you for expressing your concern."). With this simple shift, you're giving yourself permission to take up space in this world unapologetically.

instead of...	*say...*
"I'm sorry for the delay!"	"Thank you for being patient."
"I'm sorry for bothering you!"	"Thank you for taking the time to ..."
"I'm sorry I messed up!"	"Thank you for bringing this to my attention."
"I'm sorry I'm being annoying!"	"Thank you for listening."

take a compliment

Another important step in stopping apologetic behavior is to receive compliments. Maybe you were taught that it's humble not to receive compliments, but in reality, this reaction disempowers both you and the person giving you the compliment!

When you compliment someone else, wouldn't you much rather they thank you instead of saying, "No, I'm not beautiful. You are!" Sometimes I want to shake people and yell, "JUST TAKE THE COMPLIMENT! IT MAKES ME FEEL GOOD TO GIVE IT TO YOU!" When you reject compliments, you're actually rejecting the other person's feelings too. You're basically telling them that their opinion is wrong.

I know that when you're learning to love yourself, it can be difficult to receive compliments. Maybe you haven't believed positive things about yourself for a really long time. I understand. But try to resist the urge to reject compliments, even if it's for the sake of the other person at first. Over time, the more you receive compliments and express gratitude for them, the more you'll start believing them.

compliment yourself

Here's an exercise to help get you started: Give yourself five compliments and receive them. Talk to yourself like you would to a friend.

five compliments i am giving to myself and receiving from myself:

1. _____

2. _____

3. _____

4. _____

5. _____

Every time you thank someone for a compliment, you show yourself and the world that you are worthy of taking up space, getting your needs met, and being appreciated. Your self-worth muscle will strengthen by biting your tongue every time you want to reject a compliment or blurt out, "I'm so sorry!"

communicating with others

Sometimes, if I have a not-so-good day, I come home to my boyfriend and start telling him I'm so exhausted because I spent all day dealing with malfunctions on my website or getting hateful comments on social media that I'm taking to heart and are making me feel insecure. Sometimes I just want to come home and vent.

I've noticed that if I start complaining, my boyfriend goes into "fix-it mode." He starts giving me advice and telling me what he would do in my situation. He tells me to hire a freelancer to fix my website, and even offers to help pay. He suggests that I turn the notifications off on Instagram and stop opening my DMs, so I don't see the mean messages.

All of these suggestions are really sweet, and most of the time, he's right. There are things I could do to make myself feel better.

But have you ever had one of those days where you're so exhausted that you don't even want to think rationally? Like you're just not in a place to receive solutions, because you're not done complaining about the problem yet?

This is called processing your feelings! It's natural. It's normal. And everyone does it differently.

When all I want is to emotionally vent and my boyfriend tries to give me practical advice, I get frustrated, because I feel like he's not listening to me. And he gets annoyed, because he feels like I'm complaining just to complain. Do you see the issue here?

Here's a relationship hack for you: Communicate! I know you're probably giving me a figurative eye roll right now like, "Oh dear, another woman trying to give relationship advice by saying that communication is key or some other cliché like that." But hear me out.

Communication really is key. Sometimes it's easier said than done, but other times we make it a lot harder than it needs to be. And communication is not just for fixing problems in a relationship; it's also about preventing them in the first place. It's kind of like setting a mini boundary!

With my boyfriend, it's usually something simple like ...

"I had a really rough day, and I feel like I just need to vent. Would that be OK with you?"

I've made it a habit to ask for permission anytime the conversation is more on the serious side. I find questions are a lot more powerful than statements, because it makes your partner feel like they're an important part of the situation.

If he gives me the go-ahead, I tell him what my expectations are. In other words, I tell him exactly what I need/want (or don't need/don't want) so we're both clear from the beginning.

"I ask that you just listen and refrain from giving advice, because I'm really not in a place to receive it right now. Can you do that for me?"

When you tell people exactly what you need, it makes it a lot easier on them, because they don't feel pressured to say the right thing or avoid saying the wrong thing. Sometimes you just need to vent. Other times you need real advice. Or maybe you need some words of encouragement, an "I got you, babe," or a hug. When you're clear on what you need, which usually isn't much, you make life easier for everyone involved.

I do this with my friends too. One time, my best friend was sharing with me how hard online dating has been for her, how so many people on dating apps ghost her or turn out to be jerks.

My first instinct is always to give an inspirational speech about the importance of self-love, knowing your worth, and not settling for anything less than you deserve. But I've learned to stop myself before launching in, knowing that sometimes that's not what my friends need or want from me.

Sometimes your friends just want to express their feelings. Other times they want your opinion or your advice. Maybe they want you to back them up and validate their feelings. And there is a time and a place for an inspirational speech, but not all the time. I like to say something like ...

"I totally hear you. How can I best support you? Do you want me to just listen or do you want my opinion?"

It's amazing how a simple question can ease tension and avoid conflicts in relationships.

·········· **your most important relationships** ··········

If you're in a romantic relationship right now, your partner is going to play a big role in your self-love journey. Learning to communicate your needs, wants, and desires not only helps the relationship but also helps you feel seen, heard, and acknowledged. Talking to your partner about your struggles is a process of exposing yourself, letting someone into your innermost thoughts, and allowing yourself to be vulnerable.

If the thought of opening up to your partner gives you a lump in your throat and anxiety in the pit of your stomach, then either you're feeling fear of the unknown—which is OK—or you don't have a supportive partner. And if you're in a relationship you know isn't good for you, then I challenge you to dig deep right now and ask yourself, *Why am I in this relationship?* You may have a million little reasons or one main reason, but there will never be a reason that is more important than you.

Take a moment to reflect on your current closest relationship, whether that's with your significant other or a friend.

Now it's time to have an honest conversation with your closest person about your self-love journey. When it comes to talking to someone about this experience, I'm not going to tell you what to say or how to say it. Instead, I'm going to invite you to open your heart, take a leap of faith, and trust that everything will be OK.

Remember: Your partner, your friends, and your family all want to be there for you, even in your dark times. Nothing you vulnerably share about yourself will change their love for you. In fact, it might even deepen it.

SELF-LOVE CHALLENGE

talk to them

step 1: Set a time within the next week to talk to your partner or closest person about your self-love journey. It's important to plan this in advance so you don't spring it on them and both of you can be fully present and take the conversation seriously.

step 2: Open up to them as much as you feel comfortable. Tell them where you are now, why you're doing this, and what you're hoping to achieve.

step 3: Ask them to support you. I find that women have the hardest time asking for support. So many of us have a hard time asking for support because we want to be "a strong, independent woman who doesn't need anyone else" (or at least that's what I used to think). But this attitude is the fastest road to isolation, or what I like to call "lone wolfness." A lot of people think that asking for support is weak. But think about it: Isn't it a lot harder to ask for help than to pretend like you have everything handled? In reality, the opposite is true: Asking for support is a courageous act.

✦   Here are some ways you can ask your partner or closest person to support you: ✦

1.   Just be there with me.

2.   Listen to me, and let me safely express my feelings.

3.   Give me affection, like a hug, a kiss, or a romantic evening.

4.   Let me know you're thinking about me throughout the day.

5.   Send me some words of encouragement or affirmation.

6.   Call me out when you think i'm underestimating myself.

7.   Remind me of my self-love promise (see page 39) when you see me being mean to myself.

8.   Allow me to have some quiet time to myself.

9.   Emphasize to me that it's safe to express my feelings.

after you've completed your self-love challenge, write about your experience below.

quit comparing and start creating

You know when you're going about your day, feeling good, and then all of a sudden you see her ... Her on social media with her perfect body, wearing the cutest bikini, and living in the house of your dreams? Or her at the grocery store, buying organic, gluten-free crackers for her perfectly dressed kids and looking impeccable in yoga pants and no makeup? Or her at work, getting one promotion after another, always looking effortlessly put together?

You look at her and think, *She looks so amazing. She is so lucky. She is so much better than me. I wish I had what she has.*

Everyone I've ever met struggles with comparisonitis to some degree, whether that's comparing yourself to someone else or to who you used to be, who you think you "should" be, or who society arbitrarily wants you to be.

I've compared myself to others for as long as I can remember. Back in my fitness modeling days, dieting, talking about dieting, working out, and talking about working out were the ONLY things I did with my friends, so naturally, when I saw that my friend had a flatter midsection or more leg definition than I did, I couldn't help but beat myself up about not having that.

I'd think to myself, *Why don't I look as good as her? I need to try to eat less and exercise more, because once I look like her, I'll be happy. She looks so happy! I mean, I'd be happy too if I looked like her.*

I had similar thoughts about someone I followed on social media, except this time, it was all about, *Why is she getting more followers/likes/brand deals than I am?* I hate to admit this, but this person was actually someone I used to be really close friends with. It hurt that much more, because we weren't friends anymore and yet I was obsessively checking her social media stats and comparing myself to her.

It's totally normal to look at others and think they have it better or easier, because you don't see the whole picture. You don't see behind the scenes. You don't see the hard work and the blood, sweat, and tears someone endured to get to where they are. You also don't see how they feel about themselves, what they're battling internally, and if they even appreciate what they have. Even if you think you know them, there's so much you don't know. Just like other people can't see what you've gone through or what's going on in your head, you don't know what goes on behind the curtains of other people's lives either.

This is especially true when it comes to social media, because ANY photo you see on the internet is not real life. It's been carefully curated and most likely staged, altered, filtered, and edited. Plus, most people in those pictures have their hair and makeup done—either by a professional or by spending hours on it themselves—and spend hours trying to find the most flattering pose and angle. So of course you're not going to look like her when you're standing in your dimly lit closet, wearing no makeup, and staring at a mirror that doesn't automatically Photoshop you!

My point is, the comparison game is never based on reality. It is a game you play with yourself—and you never win. In doing this, you perpetuate toxic standards set by society by trying to conform to them. When you stop trying to be like someone else and focus on being yourself instead, you can actually contribute to making this world a more accepting, empowering place for everyone. When you quit comparing, you can start creating—creating your own life instead of someone else's.

And there's a totally different energy behind looking at someone for inspiration and looking at someone to make yourself feel like you're not good enough. Looking at someone for inspiration can be productive if you're learning from them, but you can't learn anything useful if you're comparing your "behind the scenes" to someone else's highlight reel.

So when you're looking at someone else and feeling sad, unworthy, or not good enough, I invite you to acknowledge those feelings with gratitude, because they're showing you where you need to look deeper within yourself. Step into a place of, "Thank you, comparisonitis, for showing me where I feel insecure and where I may need a little extra self-compassion and positive self-talk."

Then shift your focus. If the person you're comparing yourself to is online, log off and go do something else. Take a walk, read a book, or call a friend. Do anything that will get you out of your head and into your heart. Remind yourself that the more time you spend focused on them, the less time you have to focus on yourself. Remind yourself of who you are and what's important to you and focus on that. Where attention goes, energy flows, remember?

Think of comparing yourself to others as a cry for help. It's like your soul saying, "Uh, I'm losing sight of who I am right now. Can you please remind me?" Whenever you catch yourself comparing yourself to others, get grounded in who YOU are. What's important to you? What makes you different?

remember who you are

To help guide you, here are some questions to answer. It's easy to look at these and think, *Yeah, yeah. I know who I am.* But trust me, when you put pen to paper, you will discover so much about yourself that you never even thought, knew, or acknowledged. Plus, this is a great tool to come back to whenever you need an extra boost.

✦

who are you?

(For this, I like to use "I am" statements: "I am a creative and capable writer" or "I am a supportive, loving friend." It may also help to go back to the exercise in the first chapter, Who Do I Want to Be?, on page 21, and turn those words into "I am" statements.)

_____

_____

_____

_____

_____

_____

_____

_____

_____

_____

_____

_____

_____

after you've completed this exercise, write about your experience below.

_____

_____

_____

_____

_____

_____

_____

what makes you different? (write down every single thing that is different about you, your work, and your contributions to this world).

_____

_____

_____

_____

_____

_____

_____

_____

When you are solid about who you are, you can start creating. Create your life. Create your dreams. Create your happiness. And remember, who you are will evolve over time. The trick is to allow yourself to evolve into a person you want to be, not who someone else already is or who someone else wants you to be.

the little things are the big things

"Speak up, even when your voice shakes," I chanted to myself before doing my first presentation in front of my public-speaking group. I was just 18 years old, surrounded by seasoned speakers, and at this point, I'd never done anything more than a group presentation in high school history class.

In college, it took a lot for me to even raise my hand, and I rarely did. I was too scared of getting the answer wrong and being humiliated or, worse, not having enough time to clear my throat before speaking and sounding like a 12-year-old boy going through puberty.

But no matter how much it scared me, public speaking was always a dream of mine. I always thought that once I gained a lot of confidence, then I'd pursue my dreams of becoming a public speaker. Because all public speakers are confident, right?

WRONG.

The truth is that you don't need to have confidence to do the things you want. Confidence is built when you perform little acts of courage like raising your hand in class, making the first move, or asking for a raise. Real-world confidence comes from taking action even when you feel scared, insecure, and nervous.

So, at 18 years old, I gave myself permission to be messy, nervous, and imperfect while still taking inspired action. I signed myself up for a public-speaking class, even when I had no experience whatsoever. I wore a bikini to the beach, even when I didn't like my body, to prove to myself that my body-image insecurities would no longer control my life. I shared the most vulnerable parts of myself on social media before I felt ready, because I knew I would never feel fully ready. My whole career started by taking one class, wearing that one bikini, and sharing that one post on social media, because the little things are the big things. As my mentor always told me, before you sell out Madison Square Garden, you must perform at the county fair.

In the first chapter, I talked about how confidence is about your belief in your abilities. But unless you take action, you will never have an opportunity to believe in your abilities. Because you'll never see them! Doing something leads you to knowing your abilities, and knowing your abilities leads you to confidence. Once you gather the courage to speak up at a meeting once, you'll feel more confident the next time, because you've already proven to yourself that you can do it.

I truly didn't believe I could do a TEDx talk in front of 500 people (and thousands more on the internet), but I did convince myself to sign up for that first public-speaking class. I didn't believe I could accept my body at a higher weight without wanting to change it, but I knew I had to try to stop hating it. And I certainly didn't believe I could write a whole book, but I started out small, by writing a caption on social media and, well, here we are.

It's an age-old saying: A journey of a thousand miles begins with a single step.

You might be rolling your eyes right now at the cliché. But it's so true! No matter how big or small, it's the small steps that you take, that you have control over, that can lead you in the direction of your dreams.

Here is a list of little things you can do to build your confidence.
(You may want to bookmark this page.)

- speak up
- wear your favorite outfit
- sleep naked
- smile at a stranger
- tell someone how you're truly feeling
- stand up tall
- dance like everyone's watching
- make the first move
- introduce yourself to someone new
- take a selfie
- plan a solo trip somewhere
- dress for success
- take a new class
- ask for help

- help someone else
- challenge yourself
- ask questions
- accept a compliment
- give your time, money, and/or energy to a cause you believe in
- take time for yourself
- express gratitude
- show emotion
- spend money on something that brings you joy
- take responsibility
- laugh out loud
- touch yourself with love
- breathe deeply

What's one little act of courage you will do right now to build your confidence? Go do it!

when in doubt, focus out

Back in 2018, I got an email from a mom whose 15-year-old daughter, Bella, was struggling with an eating disorder. She asked me to help guide her daughter toward a positive body image, a healthy relationship with food, and unconditional self-love. At this point in my life, I didn't feel fully at peace with my own body; I still struggled with my own relationship with food (especially when I was stressed); and I certainly didn't feel like I really loved myself. I felt so underqualified for the job, because I thought, *Who am I to help somebody through this when I don't have it all figured out myself?*

I replied to her, saying that my coaching probably wouldn't be a good fit for Bella but that she should reach out to a therapist. Later that week, her mom emailed me again. She told me that her daughter was already working with a psychotherapist but really wanted additional support from me. *cue tears*

I ended up having coaching sessions with this beautiful, strong, and lovely girl for over a year, talking about insecurities, body image, her relationship with food, healing, and self-love.

I was helping her on her journey, but little does Bella know how much our sessions helped ME. Every time I sat down to video chat with her, I got to step outside of my own worries, doubts, and insecurities and be completely of service to someone else. It was no longer just about me; it became about girls and women everywhere. Bella helped me realize that.

Instead of waiting until I had it all figured out, I thought, *Let's figure it out together, Bella*. I started sharing my self-love journey, because we teach what we have to learn.

When you're feeling down, discouraged, or doubtful about this whole self-love thing, I invite you to focus your energy outside of yourself. It can really be the reset that you need. Help someone out. Call a friend just to say hi. Create something that doesn't exist. Stand in the sun, look up at the sky, and remember that you're a small part of something much bigger.

As I'm finishing this book, I'm realizing I've come full circle in this moment. My whole career started with Bella, and now I'm ending my first book with her. This is my way of focusing out, and even though I'm sharing to hopefully help you, it's also quite therapeutic for me too.

Because when you help others, you help yourself. When you empower others, you empower yourself. And when you love yourself unconditionally, you spread the gift of self-love.

bibliography

chapter 1:

Kay, Katty and Shipman, Clare. *The Confidence Code*. Chapter 1. Harper Business, First Edition, April 15, 2014.

Neff, Kristen, and Germer, Christopher. "The Transformative Effects of Mindful Self-Compassion." January 29, 2019. https://www.mindful.org/the-transformative-effects-of-mindful-self-compassion/.

chapter 4:

Wood, Alex and Linley, P. and Maltby, John and Baliousis, Michael and Joseph, Stephen. "The Authentic Personality: A Theoretical and Empirical Conceptualization and the Development of the Authenticity Scale." Journal of Counseling Psychology, July 2008. https://www.researchgate.net/publication/42739517_The_Authentic_Personality_A_Theoretical_and_Empirical_Conceptualization_and_the_Development_of_the_Authenticity_Scale.

chapter 5:

Engeln, Renee, PhD. *Beauty Sick*. Chapter 2. Harper, April 18, 2017.

Ketabchi, Natasha. "Looks That Thrill – Inside the Booming Beauty Industry." Toptal. https://www.toptal.com/finance/growth-strategy/beauty-industry. "United States Weight Loss & Diet Control Market Report 2019: Value & Growth Rates of All Major Weight Loss Segments – Early 1980s to 2018, 2019 and 2023 Forecasts." Research and Markets, February 25, 2019. https://www.globenewswire.com/news-release/2019/02/25/1741719/0/en/United-States-Weight-Loss-Diet-Control-Market-Report-2019-Value-Growth-Rates-of-All-Major-Weight-Loss-Segments-Early-1980s-to-2018-2019-and-2023-Forecasts.html.

Biron, Bethany. "Beauty has blown up to be a $532 billion industry – and analysts say that these 4 trends will make it even bigger." Business Insider, July 9, 2019. https://www.businessinsider.com/beauty-multibillion-industry-trends-future-2019-7.

Oluo, Ijeoma. *So You Want to Talk About Race*. Chapter 7. Seal Press, First Edition, January 16, 2018.

Roepe, Lisa Rabasca. "How Your Appearance Impacts Hiring Decisions." Forbes. November 1, 2017. https://www.forbes.com/sites/lisaroepe/2017/11/01/how-your-appearance-impacts-hiring-decisions/#39e8c433153d.

Kessel, Anna. "The rise of the body neutrality movement: 'If you're fat, you don't have to hate yourself.'" The Guardian. July 23, 2018. https://www.theguardian.com/lifeandstyle/2018/jul/23/the-rise-of-the-body-neutrality-movement-if-youre-fat-you-dont-have-to-hate-yourself

chapter 6:

Tribole, Evelyn, and Resch, Elyse. *Intuitive Eating*. St. Martin's Griffin, Third Edition, August 7, 2012.

"The Health at Every Size Approach." Association for Size Diversity and Health. https://www.sizediversityandhealth.org/content.asp?id=76

"10 Principles of Intuitive Eating." Intuitiveeating.org. https://www.intuitiveeating.org/10-principles-of-intuitive-eating/.

Heuer, Chelsea A. MPH, and Puhl, Rebecca M. PhD. "Obesity Stigma: Important Considerations for Public Health." American Journal of Public Health, June 2010. https://www.ncbi.nlm.nih.gov/pmc/articles/PMC2866597/. Mann, Traci and Tomiyama, Jane A and Westling, Erika and Lew, Ann-Marie and Samuels, Barbra and Chatma, Jason. "Medicare's search for effective obesity treatments: diets are not the answer." American Psychological Association, April 2007. https://pubmed.ncbi.nlm.nih.gov/17469900.

"Statistics & Research on Eating Disorders." National Association of Anorexia Nervosa and Associated Disorders. https://www.nationaleatingdisorders.org/statistics-research-eating-disorders.

chapter 7:

Brooks, A.W. "Get Excited: Reappraising Pre-Performance Anxiety as Excitement." Journal of Experimental Psychology, June 2014. https://www.hbs.edu/faculty/Pages/item.aspx?num=45869.

Burton, Neal M.D. "What's the Difference Between Feeling and Emotion?" Psychology Today, Last updated May 2020. https://www.psychologytoday.com/us/blog/hide-and-seek/201412/whats-the-difference-between-feeling-and-emotion.

chapter 8:

Schumann, Karina, and Ross, Michael. "Why women apologize more than men: gender differences in thresholds for perceiving offensive behavior." Psychol Sci, November, 21, 2010. https://www.ncbi.nlm.nih.gov/pubmed/20855900

acknowledgments

After I signed the contract for this book, I FaceTimed my mama screaming, "GUESS WHAT?!" She very unenthusiastically replied, "Ugh, are you getting married?" When I confirmed that I wasn't engaged, but instead was publishing my first book, she said, "Thank god!" and then proceeded to congratulate me. Mama, thank you for always reminding me that my potential is limitless and should never depend on a man, or anyone for that matter. You have shown me what it means to know your worth and never settle for anything less. I would not be the woman I am today without you. Also, I'm so glad you let me create an online dating profile for you on which you found Ron, the father figure I've always wanted. Ronnie, thank you for loving me as your own daughter and showing our family what it means to be a committed, passionate leader. Whether it's fixing something I've broken or giving me business guidance, I love that I can come to you with anything.

To Ilana, my biggest inspiration, you are the best thing that's ever happened to me and I love you more than I can put in words. I don't know how I got blessed with a little sister who is so funny, confident, creative, talented, caring, and wise. You embody so much pure love—I suppose I should thank Mama for making you! Thank you for being my sister (not that you had a choice in the matter), but more importantly, thank you for being my best friend. May you continue to inspire everyone around you as much as you inspire me.

To Stan, this book would not be possible without you. Well, maybe it would be, but not without permanently sacrificing my sanity. From pouring me a glass of wine during those evening (and morning) writing sessions to letting me read (and reread) sentences, paragraphs, and entire chapters aloud to you, you have been my rock through it all. Basically, thanks for letting me drive you as crazy as I drive myself. Thank you for celebrating my wins with happy dances, dinner dates, and more hugs, kisses, and cuddles than a girl can dream of. There is no greater gift than a relationship that makes you feel seen, safe, and supported. You are that gift to me, Bunny.

And of course, none of this would have been possible without my publisher, Blue Star Press. Special thank you to my editorial director Lindsay, who believed in me before I barely believed in myself. You have been an incredible support for me during the entire book-writing journey, both personally and professionally. And to Laura Lee, who worked her editing magic on my manuscript, pushing me to ditch the fluff, dig a little deeper, and take our readers further. Little did I know that a literal shot in the dark, the email I sent into cyberspace at 10:29 PM on a Friday night, would turn my dream into a reality. All thanks to the team at Blue Star Press.

Lastly, there are hundreds of thousands of people who have changed my life these past few years: every single one of you who follows me on social media, listens to my podcast, and/or comes to a retreat. You have helped me heal, grow, and make my dreams come true. And I hope that this book does the same for you.

FROM MY HEART
to YOURS,

Mary

Mary Jelkovsky is the founder of *Mary's Cup of Tea*, an online platform aimed at helping women love themselves unconditionally. After recovering from an eating disorder and healing from within, Mary started sharing her story on Instagram (@maryscupofteaa) to inspire women to ditch the diets, embrace their bodies, and find self-love. Her Instagram has over 300,000 followers and her story has also been featured in places like TEDx, Teen Vogue, and Health Magazine.

Mary is the host of worldwide self-love retreats (@retreatsbymary) in destinations like Sedona, Bali, and Costa Rica. She's also the host of Mary's Cup of Tea Podcast, the podcast that'll inspire you to love yourself.

Mary lives in Phoenix, Arizona, with her rescue pitbull and boyfriend. When she's not writing, podcasting, or hosting retreats, Mary is spending time with her spunky, confident little sister, who is her biggest inspiration.